Olive Cook

English Cottages
and
Farmhouses

with 177 photographs, 14 in colour, by

Edwin Smith

Thames and Hudson

To Norman Scarfe and Paul Fincham,
defenders of our heritage and dear friends

On the half-title page The entrance hall of Mrs Borrick's cottage, Underhowe, Grasmere, in Westmorland. Fitted cupboards, on the left, divide it from the living room in a way recalling the screen in a hall-house (see p. 90).

Frontispiece The name of Newlands Hall Farm, Frosterley, Co. Durham, refers not to the 19th century, when the new house (far right) and barns were added, but to the time some two hundred years earlier when the long-house (centre) was built on land reclaimed from the waste.

Text © 1982 Thames and Hudson Ltd, London
Photographs and diagram © 1982 Olive Cook

Printed and bound in Great Britain by Jarrold and Sons Ltd, Norwich

Contents

Foreword and Acknowledgments

MUCH PROGRESS has been made in recent years in the understanding and appreciation of vernacular buildings, for inevitably the desire to cherish and record them has been quickened as they vanish from the scene. The Vernacular Architecture Group encourages the exploration and analysis of regional buildings and publishes an annual journal, and old farm implements and complete examples of the traditional structures of the farmstead are being collected and preserved by such bodies as the Museum of English Rural Life at Reading, the Acton Scott Farm Museum in Shropshire and the Abbot's Hall Rural Life Museum at Stowmarket. Those pioneer works, S.O. Addy's *The English House* (1898) and C.F. Innocent's *English Building Construction* (1916), which first established the homes of rural workers as part of architectural history, have been followed by more intensive studies. Professor M.W. Barley's *The English Farmhouse and Cottage* (1961) traces the changes in regional houses of the great flowering period of vernacular styles, the 16th and 17th centuries, and establishes a disciplined, archaeological approach to the subject. Cecil Hewett's *English Historic Carpentry* (1980) has thrown new light upon the whole study of medieval timber-framed buildings. Alec Clifton Taylor's *The Pattern of English Building* (1962) examines the variety and uses of native materials more exhaustively and with more perception than any previous account. Dr R.W. Brunskill's *Illustrated Handbook of Vernacular Architecture* (1970) and *Traditional Buildings of Britain* (1981) describe types of vernacular buildings and regional variations and suggest procedures for systematic recording and for studying in greater depth. Nigel Harvey's *A History of Farm Buildings* (1970), though addressed to those with farming rather than architectural interests, makes a valuable contribution because it brings the story almost up to the present day and lays particular emphasis on industrialized farm buildings. *The Development of Farm Buildings in Western Lowland Staffordshire up to 1880* by J.E.C. Peters is, like Dr Brunskill's *Vernacular Architecture of the Lake District* and Professor W.G. Hoskins's stimulating Devonshire and Leicestershire studies, among those specialized surveys of a single area which are opening up so many new aspects of the regional diversity of building types. Richard Harris's catalogue to the exhibition *Traditional Farm Buildings* organized by the Arts Council of Great Britain in 1979 provides an excellent and enthusiastic introduction to the study of these structures.

I owe a great debt of gratitude for many insights to all these writers, as well as to the authors of the books and papers mentioned in the text and listed in the bibliography. The present book offers a more general and simple-hearted picture of English farmsteads and cottages and their setting, in an attempt to put a complex and unwieldy subject into a perspective of human history and endeavour. It is an imperfect picture, for not only is the choice of examples personal, but the variety, the immense richness and above all the idiosyncrasy of the material must always elude efforts to classify and embrace it in its entirety. Even the distinction between farmhouse and cottage refuses to remain firm; manor house and farmhouse are continually changing places; and the patched and altered buildings of the farmstead seldom fit into a chronological arrangement. Nonetheless it is hoped that what is written and shown here may conduce to the further discovery and visual enjoyment of a unique heritage. The photographs at least need no justification. Taken over a long period, from 1950 to 1971, they record scenes and buildings which in a good many cases have either ceased to exist or have now lost their original atmosphere and character. So these illustrations are historical.

As this is the story of the material embodiments of a traditional way of life which has now come to an end it seemed appropriate in describing individual buildings to retain the traditional names and the traditional boundaries of the counties in which they stand. New county locations will be found in the index.

My warmest thanks go to all those owners and tenants of farms and cottages, too numerous to be named individually, who welcomed my husband into their homes and who in the past and more recently have so generously answered my questions and allowed me to go into their kitchens and parlours, their bedrooms and attics, their barns and their byres. I am specially grateful to Paul Gooderham of Saffron Walden for enabling me to see the catalogues of farmhouse sales conducted by his firm during the period of the Great Depression in the 19th century; to Paul Beck for bringing to my notice documents relating to land tenure in Shropshire; to Sheila Robinson for very helpful suggestions; and to the late Reginald Lambeth, Rural Industries Organizer for Cambridgeshire, for much fascinating information about ancient beliefs and practices in East Anglia. I am grateful above all to the staff of Thames and Hudson for their support and patience, and in particular to my editor, Emily Lane, whose untiring efforts have saved me from many a blunder and have done much to improve the manuscript, and to Pauline Baines, the designer of the book, for her appreciation of the visual material.

Introduction

THE CHANGELESS CYCLE of the seasons and the rhythm of ploughing, sowing, harvesting and the breeding of cattle and sheep impose the same immutable conditions on the modern farmer as upon his Iron Age and Saxon forebears and would seem an assurance of a comforting sense of continuity. But during the quarter of a century which separates this book from its predecessor, also called *English Cottages and Farmhouses*, published in 1954, the whole structure of farming and village life has undergone a revolution which is destroying that sense of continuity as surely as it has already destroyed many of the traditional buildings celebrated in that volume. None of the upheavals of the past, not even the break-up of the manor, the long process of enclosure, or the gradual transformation of agriculture after the close of the Middle Ages from a self-supporting industry into a profit-making business, has so drastically altered the landscape of farm and field and the character of rural life.

It is sometimes said that the uprooting of the hedges, which engendered such a feeling of intimacy and contributed so much to the rich detail of the domestic English landscape, has restored the aspect of the open fields of the Middle Ages. The resemblance, even where it can be said to exist, is superficial. It must always be taken into account that open-field England was a tiny area in a vast expanse of waste, moor and forest; in the 13th century the royal forest alone is estimated to have covered one third of the whole country. The history of the Essex parish in which my own house lies and of the fields on which I look as I write is well documented, and a brief comparison of the present character and disposition of the land and buildings with their past appearance and usage sufficiently illuminates the contrast between the slow organic change of earlier centuries and present disruption, even though the visual comeliness of this particular corner of East Anglia still gives pleasure. The view from my window embraces a sweep of vast cornfields, rarely defined by a hedge or a row of self-sown saplings, sloping down to the Cam valley, then rising to pale chalky uplands on which crops grow sparsely and which might be taken for Sussex downland. Spring and autumn gales blow the topsoil from these heights so that it settles as a thick dust on sills and ledges. Here and there a copse, last vestige of once extensive forests, survives as a game preserve. Along the ridge, but invisible from here, runs a motorway and monster pylons bestride the gentle contours.

Down by the river a village of clunch, brick and half-timbered farms and cottages, a church and a mill appears at a casual glance to look much as it must have done for generations, though a scattering of council houses on the outskirts, each with its attendant car, proclaims the age, and it is symptomatic also of the age that the original villagers live in these council houses, and work for the most part in a factory a few miles away, while the cottages in which they grew up are now, sometimes smartened and 'modernized' beyond recognition, the homes of commuters or the retreats of weekenders. Like the farmhouses alongside them which have become residences instead of places of work, they have lost their connection with agricultural life. A 15th-century barn serves as an occasional theatre and social centre, other barns are used as garages, and yet another shows the tattered ribs and rotten, sagging thatch of dereliction as it sinks into a bed of nettles and rubbish.

The fields stretch in every direction enlivened only by one or two isolated farmsteads and by streams and tracks which, though their banks and verges have been impoverished by modern farming methods, are still those of the medieval landscape. One of the farms, a 17th-century rectangular house, stands on the site of an important messuage of the Middle Ages. A short straight path leads to the porch from the track, on the other side of which flint walls enclose the yard round which the traditional barn, stables, granary and pigsties were once grouped. The barn fills the whole end of the yard but now it is sheathed in corrugated iron, roofed with asbestos and linked to two huge metal silos. The granary has become a garage and beside it rises one of those enormous, windowless concrete structures which are typical of industrial 'indoor farming' and which take as little account of locality and the scale of the countryside as the silos. Behind the barn amid the debris of decaying carthouses and an old Nissen hut fragments of waggons and cartwheels, pieces of mouldering harness, an ancient rusted coulter blade and part of a light harrow with wrought-iron tines speak as plainly as the new buildings of fundamental change on the farm.

Twenty years ago hedges sheltered the fields on the western uplands and divided the undulating expanses to the east and north into numbers of smaller and more irregular fields. The varieties of trees and shrubs growing in several of these hedges – hazel, spindle, holly, oak and blackthorn – testified to their antiquity. The coverts were thicker and more widespread, a greater diversity of crops gave richer colour to the landscape and in the pastures by the river cattle grazed in the open. The splendid plenitude of nature, the countless species of birds, insects and wild creatures and the seasonal progress of plants in the hedgerows, along the paths and invading the crops, proclaimed the exquisite and precarious equilibrium between this highly evolved, mature and humanized countryside and the wilderness from which it had gradually been wrested. Neither pylons nor motorway intruded on a scene which except for the clearing of woodland, some 18th-century planting and some Victorian cottage building, had altered little since the 17th century, by which time all the fields are described as 'inclusus' – enclosed. The prospect was indeed readily recognizable as a modification of the early 15th-century landscape which was made up of a mesh of small open fields, hedged pastures and large hedged fields set amid a densely wooded terrain. The crops then included wheat, barley, peas, beans and oats. There were more scattered cottages and farmsteads at that time and more farm animals were to be seen than in this later predominantly corn-growing region: pigs, cows, horses, geese and sheep in flocks of from six to three hundred were owned by all classes of peasantry.

The fields then, as they were until quite recently, were the scene of busy human and animal activity for most of the year. Ploughing (with oxen in the early Middle Ages, later with horses), drilling and sowing, haymaking and harvesting, threshing, stone-picking, muck-spreading, hedging and ditching followed each other in quick succession during the inexorable farming year. When machines were first introduced in the last century they lightened the farm labourer's toil without immediately detracting from the animated life of the fields. Although the cutting and binding of corn were done by machines, the sheaves were still, a quarter of a century ago, collected by hand and put up in shocks or stooks in long rows down the field to create a time-honoured image of golden abundance. The threshing-machine, a big red box on wheels, took the place of men armed with flails beating out the grain on the barn floor, but men still pitched the sheaves into the machine and carried away the straw as it dropped out at the back. And the existence of the barn itself was not at once threatened; sometimes indeed the threshing-machine was kept in the big central bay. The barn was still needed for straw, and very often it provided shelter for horses and cattle.

But as technology advanced it rendered nearly all old farm buildings, old farm implements and early forms of machinery obsolete. The internal combustion engine above all, the ousting of the horse by the tractor and the huge self-propelled combine, transformed farming and the rural scene. The revolution was preparing in the 19th century when a new commercial plutocracy who had never lived from agricultural rents and were no more than superficially connected with the land played the part of traditional squires on money drawn from industry and investment. The eventual break-up of large estates, the high cost of manpower and the pressure of overpopulation accelerated the process.

By means of the new machinery corn can be threshed as it is reaped and the grain transported directly to the silos. The full catastrophic consequences of this innovation were slow to be felt owing both to a long depression during the first half of this century and to the conservatism of farmers, especially in the remoter districts. Now it has become obvious that no traditional farm building can be used for cattle and pigs where modern methods have been fully adopted and that the threshing barn, stable and carthouse are completely redundant. Farmers must always satisfy market requirements and they cannot in general preserve useless buildings representing an obstacle to profitable husbandry and a drain on resources for the sake of historic or aesthetic interest.

Similarly, because much larger fields are needed for economic working farms have been thrown together to form huge arable units, hedges have been uprooted and boundaries altered more than at any other time. Even where hedges have been allowed to survive they are brutally cut back by a machine which maims if it does not always destroy the green life tended with such skill and care for so many generations by the craftsman plashing and weaving with his billhook. The introduction of fertilizers and herbicides has freed the farmer from the discipline of the traditional rotational system, the object of which was to check disease and weeds and ensure fertility, and this has not only disrupted much of the former patchwork effect of different crops but has taken its toll of plant and wild life. An unnatural silence has fallen on the land. The giant machines visit the fields two or three times a year, devoting no more than a few days to each of the processes of ploughing, sowing and harvesting. Because the field is no longer fed on foldyard muck and because of the new methods of housing livestock, the modern farmer has little use for straw, so a few days after the combines have harvested the crops, the fields are fired. This is generally done at dusk, thus heightening the drama of an event which turns the landscape into a spectacle of calamity recalling John Martin's lurid fantasies. Sometimes every field within sight blazes, filling the evening sky with a fierce glow and the air with a menacing crackle louder than any other sound. The towering flames lap the scant remains of hedges and the few mature trees on the margins of the fields, and the following day their scorched and blackened forms exacerbate the desolation of the charred land. The former sweet wild flowers of the stubble fields, small plants which, hidden among the roots of the growing corn, only came into their own after harvest, are seen no more. The devastated earth lies bleak and abandoned until the next appearance of the machines. It was the driver of such a machine who remarked to George Ewart Evans: 'The trouble with farming today, it's such a lonely job. When I started as a back'us boy thirty years ago at least you had plenty of company!'

Though agriculture must always remain a vital factor in the life of the nation and change on the farm is in itself nothing new, the change that has taken place in the last two decades and is still going on is unlike anything which has previously transformed the landscape of Britain. It is not evolution but a complete break with tradition. Today's concrete and metal farm buildings cannot be considered either aesthetically or socially as developments of the barns and byres, the stables, granaries and carthouses of the past. So it is against a background of disintegration that the subject of this book is set. It is inevitably a celebration of the past; the present can do no more than enhance by contrast the interest of what a short time ago was still a living tradition and a manifestation of the enchanting variety of the English landscape. These pages seek to recall and record before they have gone forever some of the vernacular buildings of this country, as memorials both of the rural craftsmen who fashioned them and of the life unfolded within and without their walls during centuries of organic growth and change. They bear witness to ways of living which had altered little when most of the photographs in this book were taken, but which now, together with an older generation of farmers and farm labourers who remembered and talked to the photographer and his collaborator about the techniques and customs displaced by the machine, have ceased to be.

I
Origins and Patterns

WE DO NOT KNOW EXACTLY when our forebears began to till the soil of this island and grow crops, but the earliest traces of their fields and farms, found upon the chalk downs and high moors – remarkable patterns of cultivation such as the lynchets seen on the vast limestone expanse of Malham in Yorkshire or on Swallowcliffe and Fyfield Downs in Wiltshire – probably commemorate farmers of the Bronze Age. Excavations and aerial photography have shown that the basic traditional types of rural homestead were already established in Britain in the centuries preceding the Roman Occupation, and that they occurred in the same situations in which they were found later – in villages, in scattered hamlets, or isolated.

It is always stimulating to the imagination to come upon traces of man's earliest attempts to turn the wilderness into fruitful fields, for such gentle remodelling of the earth's surface can be seen as a continuation of the stupendous natural creative processes which have shaped the substance of the land during untold millions of years. But when, as sometimes happens, a farm, rebuilt and altered over the centuries, stands on the actual site of an Iron Age steading, its fabric as expressive as the original structure of the rock and earth beneath it, the evidence of the flow of generation after generation devoted to the raising of crops and the rearing of cattle and sheep, going on and on in that particular place despite wars and plagues and all the vicissitudes of history, takes on a significance of symbolic proportions. W.G. Hoskins describes such a farm at Bosignian in Cornwall and writes convincingly of the Iron Age beginnings of Bartingdale Farm on the east Yorkshire wolds. A little farm which in the 1960s still punctuated the immensity of the chalk undulations near Deptford, Wiltshire, presenting the typical farm image of a fort, compact and square, with thatched barn, thatched, pillared shelter for cattle, cart sheds and a haystack ranged round a foldyard within the security of thatched walls, may well have been the latest manifestation of the homestead of the many earlier generations of cultivators and herdsmen, Bronze Age, Iron Age and Romano-British, whose marks can still be made out on the surrounding plains. It may well have been the descendant of a farm like the nearby and well-known Iron Age Little Woodbury, where house, barns, byres, corn-drying racks and storage pits were similarly grouped within an enclosure. Johnson's Farm in Anstey, Hertfordshire, rises, like many another in this region of heavy clay, on a site moated for drainage as much as for protection. Excavations have revealed continuous occupation from the time of the Iron Age.

Opposite
1 Evidence of a long tradition of farming at Malham, Yorkshire, where the terraces of ancient cultivation, almost certainly of prehistoric origin, usually called lynchets, are clearly visible.

In the granite country of the south-west the impressive remains of Iron Age farming villages stand above ground to evoke the distant past and invite comparison with their successors. The tiny hamlets scattered amid the Celtic fields of a parish such as Morvah are movingly recognizable versions of the pattern created by such prehistoric settlements as Porthmeor and Chysauster. Heather mats the ruins of Chysauster and unites them with the surrounding fields and moorland, but this is the most superficial source of the obvious harmony between the eight roofless homesteads and their setting. Like all traditional rural buildings they translate the most integral component of the landscape into ordered shapes. In this case fragments of the Cornish granite, called 'moorstones', have been skilfully piled without mortar to form oval dwellings, which thus represent a stage in the evolution of the most rudimentary type of house, the round hut, from the circular to the rectangular plan.

Traces of round huts occur in many regions but usually there is nothing substantial to draw the eye. It is on Dartmoor in the vicinity of Grimspound and especially between Widecombe, Shapley and Haytor that this primitive way of living becomes a reality. Some of the countless rough shelters go back to the Bronze Age and are overshadowed by mysterious standing stones and burial chambers, others lurch among the vestiges of prehistoric fields, but all figure forth the essence of the stony waste and fill it with spectral life. It is known from the existence of post holes that timber counterparts of such round huts were common in stoneless regions during the Iron Age, and at West Harling in East Anglia a considerable farmhouse of the period has been excavated. It was circular with an internal circular yard.

The West Harling farmhouse sheltered men and animals under the same roof, and at Chysauster the single-roomed dwellings also housed animals as well as men. In a primitive society it would seem a natural and convenient solution to the problem of providing cover for animals to put them under the same roof as their owners, but the custom of sharing the house with the cow, which persisted to the present century in the wilder and predominantly pastoral country of the north and west, may also owe something to ancient beliefs. The cow helped to warm the house, and it was thought to be unlucky if she was unable to catch a glimpse of the fire. The fire protected the animal from evil spirits and encouraged a greater yield of milk.

On Dartmoor, as in the Lake District and the north, the long rectangular shape of a house occupied by men and farm animals was sanctioned by tradition and preserved by superstition, for a house more than one room wide was thought to be ill-fated. The 'long-house' was one of the basic forms taken by the farmstead. It can yet be seen, in a shape as primitive as that of the Chysauster houses, in the windowless crofters' cottages of the Hebrides and the Shetlands, and, until it finally disintegrated in the early 1970s, a farmhouse of this rudest type, ivy-clutched, its cyclopean dry-stone walls still entire, but with the mouldering thatch retreating from its rafters, stood, a Methuselah of a house, and haunted, so the villagers said, in the bleak fields on the edge of Broomley, Northumberland.

The plan of a narrow rectangle divided by a cross passage into house and

2 Barn, open-fronted
shelter and stable at
Deptford, Wiltshire, form
a compact rectangular
enclosure within thatched
walls of chalk lump, and
perpetuate an
arrangement known on
these downs at least as far
back as Roman times.

3 The Iron Age village of
Chysauster, Cornwall,
consists of single-roomed
dwellings each of which
sheltered animals as well
as men, a custom which
persisted until the present
century.

147

shippen was probably originally favoured in regions other than those with which it became particularly associated. Such a house figures in the reconstruction of the Iceni village at Cockley Cley, Norfolk, and it seems likely that at least one of the farmsteads in Anglo-Saxon Thetford was of this type. A long-house still breaks the rhythm of the street at Willersey, Gloucestershire, and an engraving of Bermondsey (then a village south of London) in Holinshed's *Chronicle* of 1585 shows a man leading a horse from a long-house. By the Elizabethan period such farmhouses were only rarely being built in the lowlands, but in the West Country the plan lingered on and in the north it became the commonest type of steading. The continuing overwhelming influence of the plan is there expressed in countless versions of that long, horizontal accent which never fails to satisfy the eye in an irregular, craggy terrain of fell and mountain. The idyllically pastoral farm in Cotterdale, Yorkshire, where the former shippen has become part of the house and another cowshed with a hayloft above it has been added to the opposite end of the building, and the low, graceful sweep of whitewashed sandstone at Dufton, Westmorland, where maroon-painted quoins, mere decoration on the expanse of wall, mark the division between human and animal quarters – both farmsteads with separate entrances for men and beasts – elaborate the inchoate theme of the Chysauster dwellings. But the archaic character of the communal roof for farmer and livestock can perhaps be even more sharply apprehended in the stark landscape of Hebden Moor, Yorkshire, where the isolated farms, which only came into being during the course of late 18th-century enclosures, are juxtaposed to shelters for sheep, wild stones heaped against the boulders of the field walls in just the same form as the Cornish Iron Age houses.

4 This farmstead at Cotterdale, Yorkshire, of the same material as the terraced landscape of limestone, sandstone and dark shale, retains the cross passage which once gave access to both house and cowbyre, and despite rebuilding is still expressive of the long-house tradition.

A tradition perhaps more important than the long-house plan for the evolution of the farmstead and cottage is to be sought in the obscure origins of timber construction. Medieval timber-framing survives in two basic forms, cruck and post-and-truss construction, the sources of both of which can only be surmised. Crucks (a word of common occurrence in early building records, found, for instance, in the accounts for the construction of a kitchen at Windsor Castle in 1236 and in the contract for a bakehouse at Harlech in 1278) are pairs of long, heavy timbers set opposite each other directly in the earth, or on a stone base, or embedded in the lower part of stone walls, and curving to meet at the ridge. The more developed crucks were made by splitting a bent trunk, thus achieving symmetry, and each pair was steadied by a horizontal tie-beam pegged into the members. Cruck construction often presents so rude an aspect that it seems as though it must embody a far more ancient practice than post-and-truss building. It does not seem too fanciful to trace its origins, as C.F. Innocent did, to primitive forms of shelter consisting of a covering of sods supported by pairs of inclining timbers connected by a ridge-pole – or 'first' (from *festum*), as the ridge-piece is called by Anglo-Saxon writers such as the author of *Beowulf*, and as it is still called in parts of Shropshire and Cheshire. The house at Thetford already mentioned was built on crucks and divided into five bays by these essential structural features. That simple early timber building was thus as firmly ordered by the idea of the bay as were the great masterpieces of architecture of the succeeding centuries and as the steel and concrete farm buildings of today still are. Bays were not uniform in size, and S.O. Addy's interesting and often repeated suggestion that their length was determined by the accommodation needed for the stalling of two pairs of oxen does not seem to be confirmed by fact. The bay lengths, for instance, in a cruck barn at Esthwaite, Lancashire, vary from 9 to 14 feet.

This atmospheric barn exhibits the form which cruck construction usually assumed from the later Middle Ages onwards. The framing of walls and roof is no longer continuous, as it must have been in the earliest examples. The crucks rise from the base of the dry-stone walls; spurs, running now into the masonry, mark what was probably the original height of the walls. Further spurs take the place of the cross tie-beams, thus providing much greater headroom, and the crucks are held together by two collars, one at the level of the second purlin, the other just under the ridge-piece. With its crudely jointed timbers and pointed arches, inevitably recalling the Middle Ages, this Esthwaite interior looks like a venerable survival. In fact it probably dates from no earlier than the 16th century, and its air of antiquity is characteristic of northern barns. Crucks had been used with more sense of design – even with a feeling for a drama – before this barn was built, as a number of late medieval cottages at Weobley, Herefordshire, show. As the carpenter's art developed the primitive curved tree principle was to inspire him with some of his happiest inventions.

Timber buildings with separately framed walls and roof may have evolved from cruck construction. In the barn at Esthwaite rudimentary principal rafters are fixed to the backs of the crucks and this could represent a stage in the gradual assumption by the principal rafters of the original

Opposite
III A half-timbered cottage with square-panelled framing at Hampton Lucy, Warwickshire. The thatched roof is extended in a steep catslide (reminiscent of an aisled hall) to cover an outshot.

7

6

5

5 The cottage in the foreground of this street at Weobley, Herefordshire, is built on the same cruck principle as the barn at Esthwaite (*right*).

6 *Right* Cruck constructed barn, Esthwaite, Lancashire.

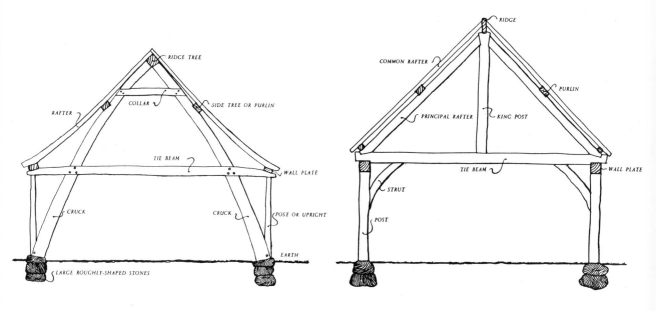

Labels in left diagram: RIDGE TREE, COLLAR, SIDE TREE OR PURLIN, RAFTER, TIE BEAM, WALL PLATE, CRUCK, CRUCK, POST OR UPRIGHT, EARTH, LARGE ROUGHLY-SHAPED STONES

Labels in right diagram: RIDGE, COMMON RAFTER, PURLIN, PRINCIPAL RAFTER, KING POST, TIE BEAM, WALL PLATE, STRUT, POST

function of the crucks. The possibility of such a connection between crucks and principal rafters is supported by a drawing in the 1899 volume of *Archaeologia Cambrensis* of a remarkable single-roomed farmhouse near Strata Florida in Cardiganshire. Of roughest rubble and unshaped timbers, it was thought to have stood since the Middle Ages; and like his medieval predecessors the farmer shared his home with cow, pigs and poultry, separated from them only by a flimsy wattle screen. The principal rafters were entirely cruck-like in form, but rose from the wall plates instead of the ground; they supported purlins and ridge-tree and were strengthened by a tie-beam. The tie-beams rested on gnarled posts, thus creating a rude arcade and aisles, and there was also a central post going up from the floor to carry the ridge-tree. In developed buildings of this type, this central post is set not on the ground but on the tie-beam and turns into a king-post; if it rests on the tie-beam and supports a collar, it becomes a crown-post.

Whether or not the two forms of timber construction were related in this way or emerged independently, it is known that aisled halls were familiar sights in Roman Britain. No remains of such structures can be seen above ground, but archaeologists have shown that they had much in common with the work of medieval carpenters. Dr I. A. Richmond unearthed farmsteads which incorporated aisled halls whose walls were framed and filled with wattle and daub and whose roofs were of the king-post and tie-beam type. As conclusive evidence is wanting it cannot be said that Roman methods survived the Dark Ages. Roman monuments, as the poem *The Ruin* so movingly reveals, filled the Anglo-Saxon settlers with fear as the

7 Diagrams showing cruck framing and post-and-truss framing.

7

work of supernatural beings. But the settlers were farmers and it would have been strange if they had not availed themselves of some of the arrangements of the Roman cultivators. The log huts and log halls excavated and reconstructed at West Stow in Suffolk, which the Saxons already inhabited before the departure of the Romans, exhibit none of the sophistication of the Roman tradition and proclaim their preference for the solid walls of split oak to which they were accustomed rather than the timber frame. But the use of the barn for living accommodation in Roman Britain may have contributed to the establishment of a similar structure as the most characteristic dwelling of the later Saxon and medieval farming landowner. A barn on one side of the quadrangular yard of the Romano-British farm discovered at Ditchley, Oxfordshire, closely resembled the later English barn with nave and aisles divided by timber pillars. Just as in the later hall-house, the aisles were used for both storage and sleeping quarters, in this case those of the farm workers. At Ditchley labourers and master were separately housed, but on simpler farms, perhaps managed by a tenant farmer, as at Clanville in Hampshire or East Denton in Wiltshire, the barn housed both farmer and workers. It is known that some of the more modest Romano-British farmsteads, such as Llantwit Major in Glamorganshire, with its barn dwelling, and Ditchley itself (except for the main house which fell into decay), remained active centres of rural labour until the late 4th and 5th centuries.

The aspect of the single-roomed farmhouse of the pre-Conquest period is still preserved in the interiors of the many aisled barns found particularly in southern England, East Anglia and parts of Yorkshire. Immediately on stepping into a barn such as that at Caldecote, Hertfordshire, the remote past becomes a living experience as it never quite does in a reconstructed building or when little of the original fabric can be seen above ground. Here at Caldecote part of one aisle has been enclosed with wattles as it might have been in the Saxon farmhouse, for storage or for livestock. The two doors confronting each other across the barn resemble those of the early hall, where one of the openings was used for animals, and at the far end of the building another door repeats that which in the hall led to a detached kitchen. Both the main doors were left open so that the draught might fan the central fire and send up its smoke to the rafters.

Looking up now in the dim interior, smoke-like shadows give substance to the image of the fire and movement to the intricate pattern of diagonal, zigzagging and upthrusting timbers overhead, a pattern which emerges as a logical arrangement following ancient practice. The great span of the sharply sloping roof must be supported not only by wall plates but by arcade plates resting on heavy posts and thus creating aisles. The posts have been shaped from tree trunks and a glance shows that they have been set inverted. According to some authorities this custom preserved the timber by allowing the sap to dry out, but the real advantage of the convention was that the butt end of the tree was thick enough for the tie-beam and arcade plates to be laid upon it, jointed to it and coupled with each other. The principal rafters meet the arcade plate at its junction with the tie-beam, thus forming a triangular structure known as a truss. In a building of this kind it is the space between two trusses which constitutes a bay. In the narrow

8

upper stages of the roof between the arcade plates and the ridge the principal rafters are tied together by collars supported by two posts standing on the tie-beam precisely at the point where it is braced by a strut slanting up from the arcade post. So an emphatic repeating pattern strengthens the rhythmic order of the bays, while down below aisle tie-beams running from the wall plate and tenoned to the arcade posts, and diagonal struts rising from the aisle tie-beam to carry a purlin over the aisle, echo and enrich that pattern.

The hall which stemmed directly from the barn-like dwelling of Saxon and earlier periods is the most significant element in the development of the medieval house. It was, however, only one of a number of types of house which had already made their appearance at the time of the Norman Conquest. In late Saxon Thetford there were small houses with a basement, which may have evolved from dwellings of the kind excavated at Sutton Courtenay, Berkshire, which were of one storey only with the floor as much as two feet below ground level. The Bayeux Tapestry shows three astonishing tiny one- or two-roomed rectangular cottages, each with a door in the middle, like a child's drawing of a house, thus achieving a symmetry which does not occur in surviving cottages before the close of the 17th century at the earliest. Little houses of this basic design can still sometimes be seen in village streets, at Digby in Lincolnshire, for instance. It may be that although no early examples of cottages like those in the Bayeux Tapestry have survived they do represent a continuing tradition. The Tapestry cottages are also unexpectedly sturdy in structure. Two of them are fashioned of horizontal planks, one is of stone and all are roofed with stone slates or wooden shingles. Like the grander houses with a first-floor hall which figure in the Tapestry, prototypes of the two-storeyed stone houses which were to be conspicuous in both town and country after the Conquest, these little cottages may be based on French example, since they must have belonged to the time immediately before the Battle of Hastings when under Edward the Confessor French influence was strong.

The Anglo-Saxons used the so-called Belgic plough, which had been brought to Britain before the Roman Occupation but was not widely known. It was a heavy implement which required eight oxen to pull it and it was capable of making a longer furrow than could easily be accommodated by the small Celtic fields or the similar fields of the Romans. This was one important reason for the establishment of the open field system. The Saxons also introduced the tradition of working the land co-operatively by means of the strip unit. A parcel of strips varying in size from about one-third to half an acre made up what was known as a furlong, and the open field comprised diverse numbers of furlongs. It is thought that the arrangement was imposed on the landscape in every region where the Anglo-Saxons settled, but many moorland, mountainous, forest and fenland territories lay outside the open field area. Cheshire, Lancashire, Cumberland and Westmorland and the dense woods of Essex and Kent knew little of the system.

The ploughing of the long narrow stretches with the eight-oxen teams threw the soil towards the centre of the strip, producing a high ridge. Each strip was separated from its neighbour by a double furrow, making a pattern of ridge and furrow which is still visible today in many parts of the country, as on the windy heights between Thwaite and Keld in Yorkshire and at South Middleton in Northumberland, a county abounding in 'lost villages', the result of the conversion of arable to cattle and sheep pastures. On a winter day when snow lies in the ancient furrows, or in the slanting light of a summer evening – such as on the occasion of my only visit there threw into relief every detail of the expanse of Goldsborough Pasture, Yorkshire – the design of long forgotten arable springs to the eye, not the straight lines of modern ploughing but graceful curves swelling in gentle waves across the immemorial fields.

9 The two-storeyed Norman house at Boothby Pagnell, Lincolnshire (see pp. 40–41).

2
The Carpenter's Art

THE OPEN STRIP CULTIVATION of the Anglo-Saxons remained the most characteristic method of farming throughout the Middle Ages, and was indeed still going on as late as the 18th century side by side with the most advanced agricultural practices in enclosed fields. Each farmer was allotted a certain number of strips, which were not adjacent to each other, so that no man had better soil than another. Even the land of the lord of the manor lay scattered among the fields of his men. Across the strips, to prevent cattle from straying into the growing crops, the farmers set hurdles. The village craft of hurdle-making was probably established before the Conquest, and it was not until after the Second World War that mass production put an end to it. Hurdle-makers, one of them a woman, were still working at Barrow in Suffolk in the early 1950s as their predecessors had done for centuries, splitting the ash to the requisite lengths and thicknesses, making the morticed holes and assembling the hurdles by hand. At that time the hurdles were destined for sheep farms in Lincolnshire and Yorkshire, for flocks had largely vanished from Suffolk. The mention of them recalls, however, the very great importance of sheep farming in the Middle Ages: without the image of the shepherd and his flock the picture of medieval agricultural life would be wanting. Wool was a major source of the country's wealth and it was at this period that the woolsack became the symbolic seat of England's Chancellor. Sheep were not confined to the specifically pastoral regions of the north, the Cotswolds and the Sussex Downs but were found on arable farms in abundance; and it was not only powerful lords, bishops and abbots who owned sheep but the peasants of humble manors who by the reign of Edward III were rearing more animals than their landlords.

Already in Anglo-Saxon England rural society was hierarchical: by the time the Norman clerks of William I were compiling Domesday Book the manorial system, which was the name they gave the social order, was completely developed. The manor comprised the whole estate; village and manor house did not necessarily coincide and sometimes the lands of a village might be attached to more than one manor. All the tenants on an estate were bound to the lord and his demesne farm (the home farm): the free tenants, later known as yeomen, paid rent for their land, the unfree tenants or serfs did weekly labour service, and all of them attended the lord's court of justice, his 'hall moot', for the settlement of their disputes and communal affairs.

The duties and payments demanded of tenants by their lords are sometimes described in medieval surveys or 'Inquisitions', which give lists of tenants and state the conditions under which they held properties. For instance in 1293 a certain Roger de Cheles of Lawton Baskerville in Shropshire rented nine acres, a little meadow and a cottage from Sir Roger Baskerville, lord of the manor, by service of 'riding with him on his own horse but at the charge of his lord'. The payment asked often seems arrestingly strange to a 20th-century reader: documents for the same Shropshire village for the year 1251 refer to rents in the form of a white rose or a white glove. The exaction of one pound of pepper is less bizarre, for in the 13th century pepper was a rare and expensive luxury and the peppercorn rent was by no means merely nominal as it is today.

The most revealing detail about the services and rents required of farmworkers is found in surveys made for ecclesiastical lords, for it was in the early Middle Ages, in the 12th century especially, that most of the great religious houses were founded and richly endowed with land. It is significant that the commonest names of farms, apart from Manor Farm, Hall Farm and Home Farm, are Abbey Farm and Priory Farm. The *Peterborough Chronicle* (published in translation by the Camden Society in 1849) contains such a record, written by Walter the Archdeacon at the time of the Abbot of Peterborough's death in 1125. Walter's account of the village of Pytchley in Northamptonshire preserves the life of that far-off time with meticulous detail:

> There are there 9 full villeins and 9 half-villeins and 5 cottagers. The full villeins work 3 days a week up to the feast of St. Peter in August and thence up to Michaelmas every day by custom, and the half villeins in accordance with their tenures; and the cottagers one day a week and two in August. Altogether they have 8 plough teams. Each full villein ought to plough and harrow one acre at the winter ploughing and one at the spring, and winnow the seed in his lord's grange and sow it. The half villeins do as much as belongs to them. Beyond this they should lend their plough teams 3 times at the winter ploughing and 3 times at the spring ploughing and once for harrowing. And what they plough they reap and cart. And they render 3 shillings at Christmas and 5 shillings at Easter and 32 pence at St. Peter's feast. And Agemund the miller renders 26 shillings for his mill and for one yardland. And the villeins render 20 eggs and the half villeins 10 eggs and the cottagers 5 eggs at Easter. Viel renders 3 shillings for one yardland and Aze 5; the priest, for the church and 2 yardlands, 5 shillings. Walter the free man pays 2 shillings for a half yardland. Leofric the smith pays 12 pence for one toft. Aegelric of Kettering pays 6 pence for the land he rents and Aegelric of Broughton 12 pence and Lambert 12 pence. And Ralf the sokeman lends his plough 3 times a year. Martin gives a penny and Azo a penny and Ulf and Lambert a penny. On the home farm there are 4 ploughteams with 30 oxen and 8 oxherds who each hold a half yardland of the home farm. There are 2 draught horses, 220 sheep, 20 pigs, and 10 old sheep in their second year.

A 'yardland' varied in acreage according to local custom between 30 and 40 acres scattered over the village fields. If the details in this account of services and rents are of exceptional interest, the names of the villagers are no less intriguing, for with the exception of Lambert they are all still Saxon and Scandinavian names.

The system illustrated by Walter the Archdeacon's survey bound the villagers together as a community and gave the humblest a voice in the agricultural policy. To a romantic like William Morris it seemed to offer a model of successful communal life. And as long as the object of each farmer was to raise food for his family rather than for the market it was economically sound. But like all human institutions it was imperfect. The feudal power of the lord of the manor pressed ever more heavily on the peasant cultivators as the Middle Ages advanced.

Although the farmworkers together formed a self-governing community their relationship to their lord was that of serfs. They could not legally leave their holdings, they could not even give their children in marriage without the lord's consent; and this system of servile tenure obtained throughout the country. Such a situation could not endure and during the 14th century the manorial economy began to disintegrate. The collapse was foreshadowed as early as the 12th century when some manorial lords adopted the custom of commuting the forced services due on the home farm for money rents, and the demesne was worked by hired men labouring all the year round instead of by farmers called off from their own strips on certain days of the week. Services were thus beginning to be regulated by money, and as money became more plentiful from the latter half of the 14th century and expanding commerce created new markets for farm produce, so land came to be regarded as a source of income rather than of feudal and military power. Revolutionary change was hastened by the Black Death. For whereas a surplus of peasant cultivators had strengthened the position of the manorial lords in the 13th century, there was now a shortage of men to till the land and the natural consequence was an acceleration of the practice of commuting labour services for money payments and a sharp increase in wages. The relation between the feudal lord and his retainers was turning into that between employer and employed, landlord and tenant.

One result of this development was that the lords of the manor gradually began to withdraw their demesnes from the village lands and to enclose them. Sometimes a lord would let the entire manor to one or more tenants, reserving only the manor house for himself. That is what Sir William Clopton did in 1410 when he let all the land of the manor of Hawstead in Suffolk to Walter Bone. Sometimes the lord would build himself an entirely new house, and the original manor house would become the home farmhouse inhabited by a tenant farmer with hired servants living in. Manorial lords also began to encourage their tenants to forego their common rights over the cultivated land they occupied and to consolidate their individual holdings and till them as separate farms.

In his *English Farming Past and Present* (1912) Lord Ernle illustrates the transformation of the manorial system by quoting the history of the manor of Castle Combe in Wiltshire from documents published in 1852. This account casts so clear a light on the process that it seems worth giving a shortened version of it. At the time of the Domesday Survey the manor consisted of 1,200 acres of arable land of which 480 acres were part of the lord's demesne. They were worked by thirteen serfs and the labour of the five villeins and the twelve bordars who occupied the remainder of the

11 A 15th-century tithe barn of Glastonbury Abbey at Manor Farm, Doulting, Somerset, seen from an open-fronted shelter. The building material – grey limestone – was quarried near Shepton Mallet.

12 This impressive early 14th-century dovecote at Sibthorpe, Nottinghamshire, originally stood near a manor house of which the only trace is a depression marking the site of the moat.

arable land. All these men were bondmen. By 1340 the village lands had increased to 1,000 acres and there were ten freemen among the tenants who held their land at fixed money rents. The rest were still bondmen. Eight of them were given cottages in return for labour services; fifteen of them farmed holdings of from 30 to 60 acres in return for some labour services and some money rents; and eleven others held 15 acres each in return for labour on the demesne. The thirty-four bondmen could, if the lord consented, buy their freedom by paying the cash value of their services as shown in the steward's book. In 1352, immediately after the visitation of the Black Death, the whole manor was divided into separate farms and let for money rents.

The pace of change was rarely as rapid as this, but by the beginning of the 16th century the relation between owners, tenants and cultivators of the land had fallen into a recognizable form of the pattern it was to assume over much of the country for the next three hundred years and more.

It is only occasionally in places such as those mentioned in the previous chapter that we can still faintly descry across centuries of taming and despoliation the landscape in which the medieval farmers toiled: it is the buildings they erected which most vividly recall their lives. Of actual farm buildings the commonest medieval survivals are barns and dovecotes. It is unlikely that a single livestock shelter of that period can now be seen, although their existence is well documented in manorial records. A farm belonging to the Knights Templars at Rothley in Leicestershire, for instance, is recorded as boasting a cattle shed that housed 24 oxen, 11 cows, a bull, 9 bullocks and 4 calves. The fine open-fronted shelter shed facing the 11 15th-century tithe barn at Doulting, Somerset, an arcade of segmental arches echoing the shapes of the barn porch arches and springing from massive cylindrical columns, may preserve the form of a medieval structure although it was built in the 17th century.

The Normans introduced dovecotes to Britain and numbers of squat, sturdy, tower-like little buildings of the early Middle Ages, either circular or square, still symbolize the forgotten privilege of the lord of the manor who alone enjoyed the right to keep pigeons. The birds grew plump on the peasants' corn until they were fit for the lord's table, a welcome alternative during the winter months to a monotonous diet of salted beef. The thick walls of the dovecotes were lined with tiers of nesting boxes, sometimes gracefully arched (like those in the plaster walls of a square, half-timbered structure at Steeple Bumpstead, Essex), sometimes consisting merely of holes opening off ledges like those making a dizzy pattern of diminishing circles inside the cylinder of the dovecote at Sibthorpe, Nottinghamshire. The pigeons reached their nests through a lantern, as at Richards Castle, Herefordshire, where later dormers also gave access, or through a louver, as at Sibthorpe. The impressive girth and simplicity of this Nottinghamshire building, the starkness of the rubble masonry relieved by but a single stringcourse, are enhanced by the isolation of the site in flat fields.

The main crop during the Middle Ages was corn and the rites connected with the harvest were among the most expressive of the festivals, public holidays and fairs which enlivened the scant leisure of the farmworker. The Harvest Supper, of which the whole farming community partook, remained an annual event in many parts of the country even after machines had replaced the sickle, and the superstitions and observances pertaining to the cutting of the last sheaf are still commemorated in some villages by the custom of bringing a corn dolly to the parish church and setting it on the screen or pulpit, on a pew or in the porch during Harvest Festival. There was no man who did not fear to cut the last sheaf, for it was the ultimate refuge of the Corn Spirit and the one who destroyed it was doomed. The sum of money awarded to him who achieved this undesirable distinction was no comfort. But once gathered the sheaf was carried, originally not to the church but to the farmhouse, tied up, decorated and sometimes dressed as a woman to preside over the Supper and guarantee the fruitfulness of the fields in the coming year. The traditional corn dolly assumes a different shape in each region, all reflecting aspects of harvest custom. Sometimes it takes the form of a miniature sheaf of corn; sometimes it figures forth the Goddess of the Harvest, the Corn Spirit; in Cambridgeshire it becomes a bell, recalling the bells of the ringers who walked in the procession headed by the harvest 'Lord' and his 'Lady' after the last load had been taken to the stockyard; in Herefordshire, Shropshire and Northamptonshire it celebrates the animals most closely associated with the harvest and appears as a mare or the horns of oxen, while the beautiful Devonshire Cross embodies the Christian imagery which was inextricably bound up with pagan memories in medieval lore.

The most important building relating to the harvest was the barn. Countless examples have survived because the design of the barn and the work that went on in it remained unchanged for so many centuries. It was as essential to the corn-growing farmer as to the stockman: the work done in the building provided the yard with straw for litter and the animals in the stockyard provided the fields with manure and so contributed to the contents of the barn. Sheaves of corn or straw were stored in the two ends of the building while in the central bay, called the middlestead, entered by double doors high and wide enough to allow the corn-laden wagons to enter, the corn was threshed during the winter months, either on a raised wooden floor of elm or poplar or on the hard earthen floor of the barn itself. The tool used for threshing was the flail, a symbol of the corn harvest, consisting of two sticks, one, the handle, fashioned of ash, and one, the swingle, half as long, made from holly, yew or blackthorn, joined by a flexible knot so that the flail would swing in any direction. Men born before the turn of the century who had used the flail and were still alive in the 1950s spoke to me of the deadly monotony and gruelling character of the work; they used to lighten the tedium by continually varying the rhythm of the swinging, sometimes achieving a subtlety rivalling that of change-ringers on the village bells.

After the corn had been threshed it was winnowed. The big double doors and the smaller doors opposite were opened wide and the grain, cast up into the draught, was separated from the chaff and bits of straw mixed with it. The men used a special wooden shovel for this process so that the grain should not be injured. A wooden sieve or basket was also used to sift out dust and small seeds from the grain. The winnowing basket was triangular in shape with a handle on either side of the apex. Such baskets have vanished except for rare examples in one or two of the new museums of rural life, but their aspect is perfectly preserved on the brass at Chartham, Kent, of Sir Robert de Septvans, a 14th-century Essex farmer.

The dusty, mealy smell of grain still pervades the dim interiors of abandoned barns, even in decay, and still proclaims the skill and endurance of the men who laboured in them. The huge dimensions of many medieval barns, sometimes, like the one at Abbotsbury in Dorset, surpassing those of the parish church, affirm their profound significance in the life of the people. The most dramatic of these medieval buildings were either monastic in origin, like the barns at Abbotsbury, at Glastonbury and Pilton in Somerset, at Tisbury in Wiltshire, or they were parochial tithe barns, like those at Cherhill in Wiltshire, Caldecote in Hertfordshire and Great Coxwell in Berkshire. From the 9th century the tenth part of the annual produce of agriculture was exacted for the support of the clergy, the fabric of church buildings and the poor; and every tenth sheaf was carried off to the tithe barn. After the Dissolution many monastic barns became tithe barns.

Though the design of all barns is determined by the use to which they were put and a basic instantly recognizable plan is common to them all, they exhibit much diversity in detail and all the individuality of local craftsmanship both within and without. The austere proportions of the vast and noble stone barn at Court Farm, Great Coxwell, accentuated rather than relieved by the extremely chaste ornament, the chamfering of the porch arches, the restrained moulding of the buttresses and the unexpectedly irregular pattern of the ventilation holes, are animated by a totally different spirit from that which radiates from the decorative barn at Abbotsbury, where the slender angle buttresses and the stepped buttress in the centre of the gable end are adorned with gay little battlements conveying a feeling of exhilaration which is irresistibly encouraged by the

quick rhythm of the closely set wall buttresses. The stone barns at Pilton and Glastonbury, carved with figures of angels and evangelists, embellished with sculptured finials, traceried windows and cruciform openings and with porches like transepts, emphatically declare their ecclesiastical origin. They are also eloquent of the easily worked limestone of the region in which they stand, just as the timber frames of the barns at Cressing Temple in Essex and the black geometry of the barns at Abbess Roding and Wendens Ambo in the same county reflect the character of East Anglia. The fronts of the last-mentioned buildings are interrupted by two or three porches, and exceptionally large structures such as these and the barn at Doulting are often furnished with more than a single entrance on the front. When barns are aisled, as they almost invariably are in East Anglia, the south-east, Hampshire, Berkshire and Buckinghamshire, and as they frequently are in Somerset, Wiltshire and Gloucestershire, the entrance inevitably takes the form of a lofty, jutting porch with a hipped or gabled roof to accommodate the harvest wagons. But in those places where cruck construction was traditional, such as Herefordshire, Shropshire and the north, the aisled barn is hardly known and then the entrance is not necessarily marked by a porch.

Though the external images of the great medieval stone barns rank in recollection with those of parish churches and monastic ruins, their stone fabric was a rare sight on the medieval farm: timber was the customary material for working buildings except in absolutely treeless lands, and in the context of this book it is the internal timber structure of barns which excites the keenest interest. Here are revealed the elements of the rapidly developing carpenter's art on which the evolution of the plan and structure of the medieval farmhouse and cottage most depended.

13 *Above left* The huge transept-like porch of the barn at Court Farm, Great Coxwell, opened onto the threshing floor and accommodated the harvest wagon. The entrance at the gable end is an unusual feature, more often found in Continental barns, where the threshing floor was longitudinal.

14 *Above* A thatched, timber-framed barn with three entrances at Wendens Ambo, Essex, built in the 15th century. The later weather-boarding protects the wattle-and-daub infilling of the framework. The wagon-sized porch doors open outwards.

35

10
8   The carpentry of the precisely ordered interior of the Great Coxwell barn
presents a refined version of the design already seen at Caldecote. It is one
found in barns of all periods. The vigorous repeating pattern created by the
pairs of diagonal struts rising from the arcade posts to support the
chamfered tie-beams and the purlins, the pleasing contrast between the
abrupt movement of these struts and the smooth curves of the aisle tie-
beam braces, the proportion of the tall stone bases of the posts and above all
the nicety of the jointing transform function into art. The Barley Barn at
Cressing Temple discloses a less harmonious and consistent design for it
was twice altered and rebuilt after it was first reared at the incredibly early
date of about 1200. But enough of the initial conceit remains to show its
sophistication. It was based on an ingenious play upon parallels and saltire
crosses, which surely must have been deliberately intended to allude to the
carpenter's patrons, the Knights Templars. Even today the interior is
dominated by the great crosses made by long straight braces running from
the arcade posts to the tie-beam and short diagonally set struts connecting
the tie-beam with a parallel beam below it. Formerly double tiers of aisle
tie-beams echoed the two tiers of main tie-beams and from the lower of
these rose great timbers duplicating the slope of the principal rafters and
crossing just below the apex of the roof. But now crown posts rest on the
upper tie-beams to support the longitudinal beam beneath the collars.

The crown-post roof is found as commonly as the type of structure seen
at Great Coxwell, generally where there is no ridge-piece. The design was
15   once splendidly represented in the celebrated barn at Cherhill which, long
in ruins, was allowed to collapse in the mid-1950s. Like the Cressing
Temple barns this building was of timber throughout, the walls
comprising heavy vertical studs filled with wattle-and-daub panels and
recalling the stave walls of the Saxons. The effect of the wall timbers inside
was to heighten the skeletal character of the giant cage of pale oak. The
structure at Cherhill was shored up by a massive long timber curving from
the wall footing up to the outer side of the arcade post, which immediately
recalled a cruck. The same use of the cruck shape occurs in the 14th-century
barn at Lenham in Kent and in the barn at Lordship's Farm, Writtle, Essex.
The builders must have been familiar with the cruck tradition although in
none of these instances is the timber fully integrated into the design.

In some late medieval barns, at Netteswell and at Little Easton, both in
Essex, posts and tie-beams consort with crucks in powerful compositions,
the cruck assuming the role of a gigantic brace passing from the wall
footing across the arcade post to the tie-beam. It used to be thought that
cruck construction was only found north and west of a line running from
Flamborough Head in Yorkshire through Sheffield down to the
Hampshire coast. But the tradition was evidently part of the repertory of
the medieval carpenter. C. A. Hewett has discovered instances of
ingeniously used crucks and forms deriving from them in the church at
Mountnessing, at Southchurch Hall and in the barn at Ladylands, Good
Easter, all in Essex. This should not perhaps cause surprise in a period
when great architectural enterprises attracted craftsmen from diverse
regions and brought them into contact with customs and methods to which
they were strangers.

Some of the most characteristic features of developed timber construction seem to have been inspired by the cruck. In the Cressing Temple Barley Barn, for example, one of the tie-beams is supported by big curving braces which are conspicuously cruck-like. The possible connection between crucks and principal rafters has been alluded to. The roof of the barn at Place Farm, Tisbury, appears as a glorious confirmation of this suggestion. For just as the famous roof of Needham Market church in Suffolk takes the fantastic shape of an aisled post-and-truss building hovering over the nave, so the roof at Tisbury assumes the form of an entire, superbly organized cruck fabrication 200 feet long raised aloft and set on top of the walls. The arched braces of the tie-beams again repeat the cruck configuration, though each is composed of two timbers jointed together to make a curve.

16

16 *Left* The tithe barn at Place Farm, Tisbury, Wiltshire, unaisled and with an arch-braced roof.

17 *Right* The arch-braced roof of the hall of Woodlands Manor, Mere, Wiltshire. Tiered cinquefoiled windbraces support the rafters.

18 *Far right* Looking upwards in the early 14th-century hall of Tiptofts, Wimbish, Essex. The arcade post can be seen at the bottom, the later Elizabethan brick chimneystack on the right (p. 96).

Crucks, through the arched braces to which they gave rise, were the source of one of the most ornamental features of unaisled buildings, the windbrace. For the windbrace is the arched brace swung round through ninety degrees and set against the rafters, to give lateral stability. Simple windbraces, crude miniature crucks, placed so that they meet to form arches below the purlin, create a decorative overhanging arcade in the tithe barn at Henley, Suffolk.

The domestic interior of the later Middle Ages, when the hall had become a status symbol, gave the carpenter an opportunity to elaborate the device. The tiered windbraces in the hall at Ashbury Manor, Berkshire, are so delicately cusped that the effect is of a narrow ribbon rippling along the edges of the arches. At Woodlands Manor, Mere, in Wiltshire, boldly cinquefoiled windbraces branch in alternating directions in three tiers to make a gigantic, wavy criss-cross pattern; while at Chapel Farm, Lingen, Herefordshire, cusped and foiled braces arch across the rafters with wild spontaneity like the antlers of a leaping stag.

The halls of these three houses, like the barns with arched braced roofs to which they are akin and like all cruck-based interiors, such as the arresting hall at Lower Brockhampton, Herefordshire, the whole character of which is determined by the giant central cruck truss, are clear of aisles and posts. It remained for the carpenter to invent a means of dispensing with the arcade posts in the aisled hall. The overwhelming, cramping inconvenience of the arcade posts in a domestic interior can still be experienced in St Clere's, at St Osyth in Essex, one of the least altered of aisled halls. The elephantine octagonal piers and vigorous arched braces, those supporting the tie-beams

meeting to form powerful arches, seem to fill the room with their tremendous presence, dwarfing and crowding out the household gods of later ages. In the Middle Ages this interior must have been yet more overwhelming, for the now open spandrels were then filled to create the impression of solid arches.

The carpenter's solution to the problem was the device known as the hammerbeam, a short horizontal timber projecting from the wall plate, supported by a brace springing from the wall post and itself carrying the post on which the tie-beam rests. This contrivance, which is characteristic of the most advanced timber roofs, makes a surprising appearance in the hall of the modest mid-14th-century manor farmhouse of Tiptofts at Wimbish in Essex, only a few years after its first occurrence in England in the Strangers' Hall at Winchester. Only one hammerbeam truss remains, for the hall has lost one of its original three bays, and this truss is blackened by the smoke and soot of the open fire which once burned where now the bulk of an inordinate Elizabethan brick chimneystack thrusts its way through the lofty room.

At the service end of the hall at Tiptofts the old aisled plan is preserved in 18 a single arcade post, once matched by another on the opposite side of the room where the former arcade has been replaced by a wall. These posts were deliberately retained to hold the 'speres' or short fixed screens which protected the main body of the hall from the draught from the doors. The speres developed into a continuous screen creating a passage – the 'screens passage' – between the hall and the doors leading to the buttery (where drink was kept), pantry (for dry stores) and detached kitchen. In spite of drastic alterations ruining the proportions of the room and exaggerating its height, the elegance of the carpentry at Tiptofts informs that bare hall with an enchanting air of spring-like freshness as potent and as palpable as that which emanates from paintings of the period, such as the Wilton Diptych, in which Richard II wears a collar of broom above his embroidered dress of gold tissue and the accompanying angels wear collars of the same broom with chaplets of white roses in their hair. Graceful roll and fillet moulding embellishes the cambered tie-beam and the capitals of the hexagonal crown posts, the arcade pier is a slender quatrefoil in section with a richly moulded capital, and cusps and wave moulding decorate the spandrels. The pier is an accomplished and perhaps intended replica in wood of the stone piers in the north arcade of Wimbish church, which had been standing for at least half a century when the Tiptofts carpenter was at work.

We have seen that many different types of houses had already evolved before the end of the 11th century. Of these the most significant for the development of the farmhouse and cottage were the long-house and the hall-house. The character of the former was implicit in the most primitive examples; the latter, chiefly owing to the carpenter's ingenuity, became the principal element in the most fruitful of domestic plans.

The two components which contributed most to the evolution of the English house, in addition to the hall-house, were the donjon keep and the type of two-storeyed stone house (with a hall on the upper floor) associated with the Norman Conquest. The tower image of the keep, whether conjoined to the two-storeyed house as at Little Wenham Hall, Suffolk, and at Markenfield Hall, Yorkshire, or set alongside the open hall, as at Longthorpe Tower, Northamptonshire, does not play a major role in the design of the farmhouse even though two of the manor houses just named were always farmsteads. Towers are often, however, conspicuous features of northern farmhouses where defence for so long remained a vital
19 consideration. At Burneside Hall, Westmorland, a 14th-century tower rises on a tunnel vault at the northern end of a two-storeyed block with a first-floor hall, which is set at right angles to a two-storeyed south wing. A decaying gatehouse with broken, roughly repaired doors of sear oak, vertical boards and strap hinges of medieval or Tudor workmanship, yields a moving view of this once grand and now half derelict farmhouse, the stone and rubble tower rent, roofless and ivy grown, the house itself encased in cement, the cusps of the mullioned windows picked out in dark red and the whole set behind the Victorian railings of a little flower garden separating the house from the triangular farmyard.

Two-storeyed Norman houses, the type of building from which both the two-storeyed blocks at Burneside Hall derived, still stand; and three of them at least, built by manorial lords, were directly connected with farming: Boothby Pagnell Manor in Lincolnshire, Hemingford Manor in Huntingdonshire (the home of Payne de Hemingford in about 1150 and continuously inhabited ever since), and the mysterious Merton Hall in Cambridge (headquarters of the King's Sheriff, lord of Bourne and several other Cambridgeshire manors). Each of these houses displays the same plan of a first-floor hall with a smaller apartment leading from it, set above a vaulted ground floor used for storage and perhaps, in the case of

Hemingford Manor, for the shelter of animals. With their striking and
sophisticated architectural detail, massive fabric, external stair – still intact
at Boothby Pagnell – leading up to the great chamber with its wall fireplace,
and two-light windows contained in the round emphatically moulded
arches of their period, they present an astonishing visual contrast to the
hall-house and a totally different arrangement.

Certain features of these little houses reappear in the plans of farmhouses
and cottages of much later centuries. The bastle houses of the Border
country, built for defence (the word is related to 'Bastille'), like those of the
early 17th century at Glassonby and Ainstable in Cumberland, repeat the
design of the Norman house in almost every particular. An external stair
leads to first-floor domestic quarters consisting of two rooms, the larger
displaying a wall fireplace, while the ground floor originally housed cattle.
Only the windows – tiny, square, heavily barred apertures in the case of the
bastle house – marked the distinction between the two structures. Outside
stairs in northern cottages built as late as the 19th century, and the stairs
leading up to the first-floor entrance of some granaries built over cart sheds
or animal shelters, as at Bibury in Gloucestershire, also recall the Norman 31
house.

Burneside Hall is one of many examples of the elaborations in stone of
the Norman plan which appeared during the 14th and 15th centuries. But
such houses were generally built only by the nobility and the dignitaries of
the Church and were considered sufficiently remarkable to be named in
deeds to indicate boundaries. They are more important for the story of the
country house than for the development of the farmhouse and cottage, and

20 Blackmoor Farm, near Cannington, Somerset.

20 only three of them will be mentioned here. Ashbury Manor, Berkshire, the hall roof of which has already been described, and the Manor House at Meare, Somerset, have both been farmhouses since the Dissolution of the Monasteries. Blackmoor Farm, near Cannington in Somerset, a late 15th-century manor house, has always been associated with husbandry. Abbot

22 Adam de Sodbury of Glastonbury built the Meare house as a summer retreat in about 1330. It unites two two-storeyed houses set at right angles to each other; a projecting porch on the main front resembles that which by this time usually sheltered the entrance to a hall-house and is placed in the position which in a hall-house marked the screens passage. The figure of an abbot rising from the gable of this porch still announces the ecclesiastical origin of the farmhouse and mossed buttresses dividing the bays, the ghost of a huge Gothic window emerging from the blotched masonry of the façade, and the tall, cusped lights of the noble windows of the rear heighten the disparity between the early and more recent history of this gaunt relic. The great upper hall illumined by those Decorated windows, where the Abbot and his attendants lived in splendour, served the farmer's wife of the 1950s as a lumber room. On entering it one looked towards the magnificent fireplace with its tall five-sided moulded hood and swelling corbels across a surreal assortment of junk – discarded toys, among them a headless baby doll; an old pram; parts of bicycles; one or two broken farming tools; a pile of apples; a heap of rags; and a decrepit, sagging upholstered armchair.

Ashbury Manor was the creation, more than a century later, of another Glastonbury prelate, Abbot Selwood. The builder started with an older house and added another range in line with it containing a lower and an upper hall. An almost centrally-placed porch led into a screens passage between the new range and the original building, which became the pantry, buttery and kitchen. This is a very early instance of the incorporation of the kitchen in the domestic plan. A short arm at the rear consists of a small chamber on each floor, a garderobe or lavatory (a feature which is only found in grand houses), and a spiral stair, a form of staircase which was introduced by the Normans and is essentially connected with stone buildings.

Blackmoor Farm consists of three two-storeyed blocks and the patched and weatherstained exterior remarkably preserves its medieval aspect: the windows with their ogee-headed lights survive unaltered and the projecting porch is still furnished with its original outer and inner doorways. The house has slightly changed inside; it had a central double hall, one on each of the two floors, while one of the cross blocks comprised a tall chapel and a two-storeyed antechapel (the upper floor of which was reached by a spiral staircase), and the other, projecting at the rear of the house, contained the kitchen with a chamber above it. So Blackmoor Farm already embodies the plan which was to emerge from the fusion of the Norman house and the open hall.

21 *Above left* The upper floor of the two-storeyed manor house at Ashbury, Berkshire, is reached by a stone spiral staircase with a newel column at the narrow end of the steps.

22 *Above* The rear of the 14th-century manor house, Meare, Somerset.

21

20

43

It was this combination of the two-storeyed house and the single-storeyed hall in the commonest of structures, the timber-framed house, that led to the most significant developments in the plans of farmhouses and cottages. At Little Chesterford Manor, Essex, a replica of Hemingford Manor was built of flint rubble and clunch in about 1225 and an aisled hall was set at right angles to it some seventy years later. During the 14th century a two-storeyed cross-wing, similar to the original stone house in shape but timber-framed, appeared at the opposite end of the hall, turning the design into the H-plan which was to dominate farmhouse building for generations. The house at St Osyth, the hall of which has been described, is timber-framed throughout and is a classic example of the early H-shaped house comprising a one-storeyed hall flanked by two-storeyed cross-wings. The ground floor of the wing to the right of the screens passage (marked by the entrance) was used as buttery and pantry and the room above it, reached by a simple ladder, served for storage. The ground-floor room at the other end of the hall was called the 'bower' or 'chamber', although both terms might also be applied to the upstairs room, which was also known as the 'solar'. By the last quarter of the 14th century, about twenty-five years after St Clere's was built, the word 'parlour' had come into use for the lower room. When Pandarus visits his niece in Chaucer's *Troilus and Criseyde*, written in about 1380, he finds her with two ladies in her 'paved parlour'. When, in the same poem, Chaucer refers to the 'chambre' it is of a bedroom he is speaking.

Bower and hall, again according to Chaucer, seem to have been as much part of the poor cottage as of the manor farmhouse. In the *Nun's Priest's Tale* the poet says of the widow's 'narwe cotage', 'ful sooty was hir bour and eek hire halle'. Poor though she was this widow had three large sows, 'three keen and eek a sheep that highte Malle', and

> Hir bord was served moost with white and blak, –
> Milk and broun breed, in which she found no lak;
> Seynd bacoun and somtyme an ey or tweye.

Even in such a humble dwelling the animals were separately housed and shared a yard with Chaunticleer the cock and his seven hens.

At St Clere's a lean-to adjoins and enlarges the service wing. This modest addition to the plan became part of the idiom of farmhouse and cottage building in most regions. In 16th- and 17th-century cottages and often in much later examples it constituted the only service room. Variously known as the 'outshot' or 'outend', or, in some parts of Kent (according to inventories in the Maidstone Record Office), the 'cove', the form of the lean-to may have been suggested by the hall aisle.

The heavy timbers of houses such as St Clere's were framed on the ground, the timbers being marked with Roman numerals, and then 'reared' into position, a formidable task in which the help of neighbours was essential. Records refer to payment for meat and drink to villagers for their pains. In 1420 twopence for drink was given to each of the men of Alford in Somerset who had assisted at the 'reryng' of a house in that village. (Framed houses could, if necessary, be easily dismantled and moved. In 1377 a hall-house with two chambers was taken in Surrey from Wimbledon

to Shene, and in the 15th century a hall was moved from the manor of Thundersley and re-erected at Rayleigh Park, Essex. In our own century Sir Edwin Lutyens transferred the hall of a house at Benenden, Kent, to Northiam in Sussex, where it became part of Great Dixter, and in recent years the magnificent abandoned barn at Wherstead, Suffolk, was removed to another county and converted into a house.) The spaces between the timbers were commonly filled with wattle and daub, the daub composed of a mixture of clay, dung and chopped straw, laid on rods fixed horizontally in grooves in the sides of vertical, closely set timbers or, when the panels are wider, on a basketwork of upright staves, usually of oak, and horizontal rods of hazel or ash. The panels were often finished on each side with a thin coat of plaster composed of lime, sand and cow hair, which offered more resistance to the weather than daub. If left uncovered, the daub tended to shrink.

The strong influence of the traditional plan of a hall with one or two cross-wings can be detected in the streets of most of the villages and small country towns in regions where timber-framing survives. Again and again groups of two or more cottages catch the eye which clearly started life as halls with cross-wings. Sometimes the former hall may remain one-storeyed, sometimes – as in a house at Linton, Cambridgeshire, now divided into two cottages – a dormer window shows that a floor was

23 Cottages at Linton, Cambridgeshire, once part of a single house, the design of which is recognizably the same as that of St Clere's (Pl. II) despite later alterations, the most important of which was the lateral division of the hall to create an upper storey, lit by a dormer.

23

inserted at a later date. Houses built at the end of the 16th and during the 17th centuries and designed as two-storeyed structures from the beginning still conform to the familiar plan of a central block either with a single or with two cross-wings. Anyone walking or even driving through almost any East Anglian village will encounter several examples, each now generally become two or more cottages or perhaps a little shop and cottages. In some of these houses the ridge of the two-storeyed hall block

53 rises above the ridges of the cross-wings, thus reversing the arrangement
II seen at St Clere's and in other early hall-houses, where the cross-wings considerably overtop the hall.

Very often it is the side wall of a single cross-wing which fronts the
5 street, while the former hall is at the rear. A number of houses at Weobley, Herefordshire, present their cross-wings to the street, and the conspicuous front, decorated with carving, of a house in Saffron Walden, Essex, now the Eight Bells inn but once a farmhouse, is the wall of a cross-wing attached to a one-storeyed hall built under the same roof as a barn, like a long-house, and facing what was the stockyard.

23 The projection of the cross-wings of the house at Linton is noticeably slight by comparison with those of an early house like St Clere's, and the roof line is continuous. The carpenter was making continual modifications in the conception of the timber-framed house to bring it ever more in line with the two-storeyed stone houses of the wealthy. His endeavours were prompted by the growing needs of tenant farmers, whose welfare was a special concern of Henry VII after two centuries of agricultural unrest, but who could rarely afford to build in any material but wood. An important step towards the achievement of a compact design had been taken when the hall was cleared of its aisles, for the pitch of the roof then became less steep
II and the eaves line much higher. A comparison of the exterior of St Clere's
I with that of Lower Brockhampton Manor illustrates the way in which this change began to reduce the original sharp differentiation between hall and cross-wings.

The next stage in the development of the timber-framed house was to align the walls of hall and cross-wings. To this end, the ground-floor walls were commonly brought into line, while the cross-wings were marked only by their gables and an upper projection depending on a feature known as
24 the jetty, which became popular during the 15th century. A number of explanations have been put forward to account for this development: it has been described as a means of enlarging the upper room, as a method of preventing the floor joists from sagging, and as a protection for the foundations of the house. The most obvious advantage of the device is that it strengthens the timber framework by providing two places instead of one for jointing the ground- and upper-floor posts with the first-floor sill beam. Yet it seems unlikely that the carpenter was consciously striving for any of these advantages. In all creative activities new ideas arise spontaneously in the course of the work, and probably it was when laying the joists to support the floorboards of an upper storey that the visual as well as the practical possibilities of the jetty sprang to the carpenter's mind. It was a way also of marking the existence of what had become important rooms. The decorative opportunities afforded by the oversail must have made a

24 Jetty with moulded fascia board and corner post supporting the dragon beam at Clavering, Essex.

special appeal in an age when the carpenter's craft had become a superb art, transfiguring the roofs of East Anglian churches with visions of flying angels, quickening the mystery of sanctuary and chapel with the delicate filigree of vigorously branching screens, and animating choir stalls, benches and bosses with teeming imagery as expressive of the pageantry of nature as of the abiding influence of the supernatural.

The jetty was not only ornamental in itself: the timber sill of the upper wall above the jetty (the bressumer) provided a splendid expanse for a running motif. At Baldwin's Manor, Swaffham Prior, Cambridgeshire, the bressumer of the cross-wing, which faces the street with the hall at the rear, is embellished with a scroll-and-fillet ornament; and examples at Saffron Walden show battlements and vines and rose tendrils with birds of the fields and hedges peeping from the leaves. Sometimes the projecting ends of the beams of a jetty are covered by a fascia board and this again may be carved, as in a row of cottages, once a single building, at Clavering in Essex. If the upper storey oversails the lower along the façade and on an adjacent side, as it does at Clavering, two sets of joists must be set at right angles to each other and to this end a stout beam called the dragon was fixed diagonally across the floor. Where it projected at the corner of the house it was supported by a corner post, an obvious place for the display of the woodcarver's talent. The sensitive shaping and moulding of the reeded shaft, tall gently curving bracket, and square capital of the bleached, silvery post at Clavering remain tremblingly alive after five centuries of attrition.

Another feature of the timber-framed house which the carver found irresistible was the bargeboard, a late 15th-century innovation, fixed to the ends of a gable a short distance from the face of the wall to protect the roof timbers from the effects of the weather. The bargeboards of the gatehouse and cross-wing at Lower Brockhampton are enlivened by firmly carved trailing vines, and at Weobley the bargeboards flaunt bold quatrefoils, undulating ribbons and scallops.

When the bay window or oriel made its first appearance in the later Middle Ages, to indicate the presence of a solar in more substantial farmhouses, it was supported by a wooden bracket which gave the carver sufficient space for a figure composition. At Newport, Essex, where the base of an oriel is corbelled out of a single balk, the craftsman's chosen theme was the crowned Virgin holding the Child and brandishing a sceptre between two angelic musicians (an organist and a harpist), cut in deep relief with an eager rapture stronger than erosion, cracks and weather stains.

This house at Newport is noticeable by comparison with all the others so far seen for the absence of gabled cross-wings. The eaves line of the oversailing storeys is continued over the recessed hall by means of braces curving from the wings. This compact form of hall-house is known as the 'Wealden' type, and is popularly associated with the Weald of Kent and Sussex. A particularly complete and polished example stands at Goudhurst – Pattenden Manor, named after its first owner who built it in about 1470. Although the hall of Pattenden was open to the roof in the 15th century

25 Oriel in the jettied upper floor of one wing of a 'Wealden' house at Newport, Essex.

the front and back doors and the screens passage between them were not in the hall but in the north wing, under the floor of the upper room; thus the screen did not project into the hall at all but stood flush with the wall above it. The space had already in fact become what in much later plans is known as the 'hall', that is the entrance hallway. The Newport house is proof that the Wealden plan was not peculiar to the Weald. Groups of cottages in Bridge Street and Castle Street, Saffron Walden, were built as single houses to this design; and a house as far away as Stratford-on-Avon, Warwickshire, takes this form.

The end of the story of the metamorphosis of the hall-house into a dwelling which was two-storeyed throughout belongs to the following chapter and to the period when chimneys became an essential feature of domestic building. That period also saw the full flowering of vernacular styles. Of course where builders could only resort to local materials differences became manifest from the beginning. The stone slates, for instance, which cover the vast roof expanses of the barns at Great Coxwell and Pilton are as eloquent of the limestone of their regions as is the fabric of their walls. And the distinction in style between the aisled barns found eastward from Wiltshire and in the south-east, and the unaisled barns of the west, has been observed. But even though in their homeland crucks give aggressive individuality to some houses of the late Middle Ages, as at Weobley, there were few sharp distinctions before the 16th century in the most widespread of all forms of medieval farm and domestic building, the timber-framed. The cross-wing at Lower Brockhampton does indeed hint in a rudimentary way at the special decorative tradition of this part of the country, which was to reach its amazing culmination in the Elizabethan age. A roundel fills the apex of the gable and closely set studs consort with

26 At Pattenden Manor, Goudhurst, Kent, a typical 'Wealden' house, the three units of the hall-house are still distinct but, covered by a single roof, they begin to assume a rectangular plan.

49

square panels. But closely set studs distinguish not only the gatehouse of
Lower Brockhampton but the houses at Newport in Essex and Goudhurst
in Kent just examined. And square panels were common in districts other
than the West Midlands in the Middle Ages. They can be seen, for instance,
at Biddenden in Kent, Fittleworth in Sussex, Cerne Abbas in Dorset,
Dorchester in Oxfordshire and even at Banks Green in Essex. Timber-
framed houses pictured in contemporary manuscripts, such as the Bedford
Book of Hours, are invariably square-panelled, and this must surely
indicate that idiosyncrasies of style had yet to develop.

Very little has been said about the dwellings of the lord of the manor's
poorest tenants, and for good reason, for no medieval peasant's cottage
survives. Many of them were doubtless so insubstantial that they could be
erected or demolished as readily as tents, for it was a common cause of
complaint in the Middle Ages that villeins absconding from their manors
would take down their houses and carry off the fabric to set it up in their
place of refuge. But writers like Chaucer and the author of *Piers Plowman*
tell us something of village homes in the Middle Ages, and tax assessments
which were based on personal property throw light on the size and contents
of the humblest houses of some areas. M. W. Barley quotes the assessments
for the town and neighbouring villages of Colchester in Essex for the years
1296 and 1301. Peasants' houses seem to have consisted of one or at most
(like that of Chaucer's widow) two rooms, and the contents appear not to
have amounted to more than one or two beds and a few cooking
implements such as an andiron, a brass posnet (a forerunner of the
saucepan, fitted with short legs) and a tripod. A trestle table known as 'the
board' and a cradle are mentioned in *Piers Plowman*.

More is known of the furniture, goods and chattels of wealthy
households. Inventories of well-appointed farmhouses like that of the
Pastons at Hellesdon in Norfolk list trestle tables, benches, stools,
cushions, a principal bed with a headpiece and canopy, truckle beds which
in the daytime were kept under the big bed, chests for clothes, a cupboard
for food called the 'aumbry', pewter and brass pots and pans, gridirons,
candlesticks, silver spoons, marble pestles and mortars and one or two
spits. A stool with a jug on it and a chair (which was a rare article of
furniture) with large carved leaves bursting from the supports occur on a
misericord in Screveton Church, Nottinghamshire, where a man is shown
warming himself at a wall fireplace.

The hangings in the Pastons' house were of a fine cloth called 'say',
resembling serge. A cheap and popular form of wall decoration was the
painted cloth, a canvas stretched on a wooden frame. Such hangings came
into fashion at the end of the Middle Ages as a substitute for the tapestries
of the nobility, and by the mid-16th century even a farm labourer living in a
two-roomed cottage might boast of one. They must have been the work of
itinerant painters. The cloths are now rare and no medieval example can be
seen. A late 16th-century set in the Luton Museum, Bedfordshire, religious
in subject-matter, shows the affinity with tapestry design; and a series of
Elizabethan wall paintings from Hill Hall, Theydon Mount, Essex (now in
the Victoria and Albert Museum, London), is executed in the manner of
cloth paintings and is also clearly intended to imitate tapestry.

Opposite
27 Wall paintings at
Piccott's End,
Hertfordshire, discovered
in 1953.

Opposite
IV Thatched cottage
made of chalk lump at
Little Sampford, Essex.
Oak shingles above and
below the dormers may
indicate that the entire
roof was once shingled.

V *Overleaf* Thatched and
clapboarded cottage,
Anstey, Hertfordshire,
recalling the small
farmhouses recorded in
16th- and 17th-century
inventories. (See
pp. 84–85.)

Paintings done directly on the plastered walls were as much favoured as cloth paintings in the late Middle Ages and the vogue persisted until the mid-17th century. A painted room of about 1500 was discovered under layer upon layer of wallpaper in the upper room of a wing of a very modest house at Piccott's End, Hertfordshire. The subjects, as might be expected, are religious, and those which are best preserved are reminiscent of a triptych, the panels of which are divided by the studs of the timber frame, though the artist has carried his background design of coiling vines of great size right over the timbers. A full-length figure of the Salvator Mundi fills the central panel; to the left is a Pietà and to the right the Baptism. The huge ochre cross behind the Virgin of the Pietà bears the word 'FÜRST', which suggests a German source for the paintings. Perhaps they were based on a German woodcut of the period. Crude though the work is, its coarseness accentuated by the lumpiness of the wattle-and-daub infilling under the plaster, the dynamic indigo outlines, the expressionist drawing and the white, ochre and vermilion of the colour scheme convey an extraordinary vehemence of feeling. These paintings in these unpretending domestic surroundings bring us abruptly into contact with an attitude of mind to which we have long become strangers, an attitude which pervaded all the activities of the Middle Ages but which at the very time the painter was at work on these panels was rapidly changing to embrace horizons far beyond the confines of the medieval world and to bring about electrifying developments and mutations even in the traditional, rural buildings of which I am writing.

3
A Vernacular Art at its Zenith

WHEN THE 16TH CENTURY OPENED the landscape looked much as it had done a hundred years earlier: the population, still barely 3 million, was thinly scattered in the north and for the most part lived in the belt of country lying between the Wash and the Thames and running in a south-westerly direction to the Severn. Fell and forest, moor and marsh covered many more square miles than field and farm, spicing the life of town and village with a sense of mystery and adventure. But the profound change in outlook which divided medieval from Renaissance England, a change symbolized by the Dissolution of the Monasteries, the establishment of the Church of England and the translation of the Bible, was soon reflected in the aspect of the countryside and in attitudes to farming. The 18th century was the great age of revolution in farming practices, but that revolution was set in motion two hundred years earlier. The glimpse of conditions in the later Middle Ages afforded by the previous chapter showed that the almost static organization of medieval agriculture, so deeply expressive of the religious experience of the period, was already undergoing a transformation. But now, at a time of which every manifestation bears the impress of extraordinary, irresistible impetus, the transition to a form of agriculture based on money and markets rather than on services was rapid and concentrated. The medieval village and manor farms supplied the wants of their own communities: the aim of Tudor and Elizabethan farmers and their successors was not merely to satisfy their own needs but to raise cattle and crops for profit and to accumulate industrial wealth.

The new lively interest in farming and the growth of the conscious desire to improve methods led to the appearance of an agricultural literature and of manuals of instruction. *The Boke of Husbandry* by John Fitzherbert, a Catholic of Derbyshire and an expert breeder of horses, was published in 1523 and reprinted a number of times during Elizabeth's reign. It describes the writer's own procedures and practical experience, with frequent reference to old sayings and country lore:

> He that hath both sheep, swine and hive
> Sleep he, wake he, he may thrive.

Fitzherbert exhorts the farmer to oversee everything himself and to keep in his purse a pair of tablets on which to write down anything amiss when on his rounds. If he cannot write 'let him nicke the defautes upon a sticke'. The young farmer is advised to 'gette a copy of this presente boke', learn it by heart and 'according to the season of the yere, rede to his Servants what chapter he will'.

Opposite
VI A thatcher at work, Sheepwash, Devon. (See p. 104.)

Thomas Tusser, better known today and in his own time more popular, was a musician, trained as a choir boy in the chapel of Wallingford Castle, but he farmed all his adult life at Brantham in Suffolk, where the house he lived in still forms part of Brantham Hall Farm. It was there that he introduced the cultivation of barley, hitherto not grown in that district, and there that he wrote his *Hundred Points of Good Husbandry*, expanded sixteen years later, in 1573, to *Five Hundred Points of Good Husbandry*. Tusser uses hypnotically jogging rhymes and rhythms which seldom betoken a musical ear:

> Take verjuice and heat it, a pint for a cow,
> Bay salt, a handful, to rub tongue ye wot how;
> That done with the salt, let her drink of the rest,
> This many times raiseth the feeble up beast.

Nevertheless the whole book springs from the writer's personal knowledge of farming and great love of the land and reveals a most endearing character – kindly, tolerant and generous, fond of old traditions, rejoicing in the festivals which enlivened the farmer's year, and yet, like so many Elizabethans, always mindful of the brevity and uncertainty of life.

Tusser tells of the farmer's skills and of his seasonal labour. He informs us when crops should be sown, and points out that different grains should not be grown together though they may be mixed before being sent to the miller. So indeed they were in the 16th century, for the most commonly eaten bread, called 'maslin', was baked from a mixture of wheat and rye which in times of dearth might be diluted with barley, peas, beans and lupins. The land must be prepared for winter crops, says Tusser, by three ploughings, in autumn, spring and summer. Apples must not be gathered until after Michaelmas; in autumn rams and young bulls must be gelded and stable and cowhouse put into good repair; and at that season too Cisley, the dairy wench, must clean out the boar's pen 'for measling [tapeworms] and stench'. In October the thresher must begin work in the barn and sloes are gathered. From November onwards beasts are occasionally killed and beef, bacon and mutton are all hung in the chimney to dry in the smoke of the fire. Green peas must be sown at Hallowtide, runcivals (marrowfat peas) at Candlemas. Hedging and ditching are the chief outdoor work of December, and this month is cheered by the great Christmas festival of fire and light, of new beginnings and lengthening days. Tusser's homely picture of the twelve days of rejoicing, of the thronged hall decked with holly and ivy, of the bringing home of the yule log, the play of the mummers, the dancing and singing, the zest of the instrumentalists and the feasting, puts one in mind of the marvellous celebration of the season's rites, unaltered after more than three hundred years, in Thomas Hardy's *Under the Greenwood Tree* (1872). Both descriptions have an affinity with the earthy paintings of the Dutch School.

> Beef, mutton and pork, shred pies of the best,
> Pig, veal, goose and capon, and turkey well dres't,
> Cheese, apples and nuts, jolly carols to hear
> As then in the country is counted good cheer.

Tusser does not mention Christmas puddings, for they did not make their appearance until about 1670. Turkeys had only been introduced into England about ten years before the publication of Tusser's 1557 edition.

The routine of the 16th-century arable farmer in a region remote from East Anglia is minutely recorded by a contemporary of Tusser's, a Cornishman, William Carnsew of Bokelly, who kept a diary for the year 1576–77. It is naturally a more personal account than Tusser's, but the routine of the two farmers is remarkably similar. Yet another writer, Leonard Mascall, a Sussex man, compiled the *Government of Cattell* in 1591, dealing with the diseases of animals. In the following century Gervase Markham not only wrote a number of instructive volumes about all branches of husbandry but provided plans for a convenient farmhouse which was to include a great hall, a dining parlour with an 'inward closet' for the mistress's use, a stranger's lodging 'within the parlour' and a buttery, kitchen with room for brewing, a dairy and a milk house. Henry Best specialized in the farming methods of his native Yorkshire and Sir Hugh Platt and Edward Maxey concentrated on ways of sowing seed other than by hand broadcasting.

Special crops were grown for the market. The huge London market – the capital numbered about 200,000 by the end of Elizabeth's reign and by the time of the Restoration included almost a tenth of the $5\frac{1}{2}$ million inhabitants of England – commandeered butter from Suffolk, cheese from Cheshire, cider from Devon and Hereford, and cattle from the north. The best flax and hemp came from Lincolnshire; madder and saffron for cloth dyeing were concentrated in Essex; hops, introduced from the Low Countries, were being cultivated by the middle of the 16th century, not just in Kent, with which they were particularly associated later on, but in Worcestershire, Essex, Yorkshire and Cornwall. Tudor farmers used improvised maltkilns as drying rooms for the hops, sometimes built in the back of a chimney, but early in the 17th century the group of traditional farm buildings was invaded in the areas mentioned by the conspicuous shape of the tall, rectangular oasthouse with a brick drying floor.

The devotion of different regions to the crops they grew best instead of to subsistence farming was one small instance of the delight in diversity and individuality which marked the inquiring energetic spirit liberated by a changed habit of mind. And this was not the only way in which it found expression in the practical world of farming. Certain localities began to be known for special breeds of farm animals, described by the Rev. William Harrison in 1577 (in his *Description of the Island of Britayne*) as unrivalled for size and beauty, and hardly recognizable as the same species as the scrawny, stunted sheep and cattle of the Middle Ages depicted in such manuscripts as the Luttrell Psalter. Long-horned oxen, black with big white horns tipped with black, were raised in Yorkshire, Derby, Lancashire and Staffordshire, while the ancestors of the modern shorthorn, pied with white and with crooked horns, were bred in Lincolnshire. Leicestershire and Northamptonshire became famous for their cattle. Small-boned, black-faced sheep were associated with Herefordshire and Shropshire; the Cotswold breed, which gave its name to the hills – 'the wolds of the sheepcotes' – was already long-woolled and distinct; and the sheep of Yorkshire and the north were satisfying an increasing demand for coarser wool. The 'great horse' which was to give rise to the mighty shire horses of later ages occasionally found its way into the farmyard, after stallions imported from Naples, Germany, Hungary, Friesland and Flanders had encouraged the breed. But it was only after body armour was finally discarded in the 17th century that the really heavy horse was able to show its mettle on the farm.

Familiar crops were enriched by new varieties. Wheat might be white, red, main (a mixture of white and red), Turkey or Pinky, grey, flaxen, pollard, English or peak; barley was of three kinds: sprot, longear and bear or big; oats were red, black or rough; and there were white, green, grey and runcival peas. A new crop, buckwheat, was introduced from Russia and North Germany: it was described in the *Four Books of Husbandry* by the Dutchman Heresbach, translated into English in 1577 by Barnaby Googe, a Lincolnshire farmer and poet. Googe was the first person to recommend the growing of trefoil and clover for pasture. He also stressed the importance of manure and designed a novel reaping machine. In the mid-17th century a Worcestershire farmer, Andrew Yarenton, grew clover and wrote a manual about it, *The Great Improvement of Lands by Clover*. Some thirty years earlier Sir Richard Weston had grown turnips on his Surrey farm as a field crop and had thus inaugurated the cultivation of root crops which, developed by the Georgian pioneers of improved farming, led to entirely new systems of husbandry. Robert Loder, a yeoman who lived in Berkshire at Prince's Manor Farm overlooking the Vale of the White Horse, experimented with different manures, including malt dust; by ploughing in a crop of autumn corn that had failed, he got a yield as high as the national average in the first half of the present century.

Robert Loder's innovations and something of his vigorous, determined character and his eagerness for financial gain are revealed in his fortuitously preserved farm accounts. There were no doubt many others of like energy and resourcefulness, especially among the new and prosperous class of yeomen farmers who were responsible for more than a hundred acres. Yeomen were defined by Bacon as 'the middle people between gentlemen and peasants'. They constituted a class which had come into being as a result of the social changes which followed on the Black Death. Among them were not only freeholders such as Robert Loder but lessees for lives and copyholders, who paid a nominal yearly rent and a fine when the land passed from father to son. They were called 'copyholders' because the transfer of their property was entered in the Court Roll of the manor and their title was secured by their copy of the Roll. Latimer's father was a yeoman of this kind: he had no land of his own and rented his farm at £4 a year. Harrison describes the yeomen as 'for the most part farmers to gentlemen' that by attention to their business 'do come to great wealth insomuch that many of them are able and doo buie the lands of unthriftie gentlemen'. Harrison also says that they 'commonlie live wealthilie, keepe good houses' and had 'learned also to garnish their cupboards with plate, their joined beds with tapistrie and silke hangings, and their tables with carpets and fine naperie'.

The importance of the yeoman farmer is underlined by such specialist authors as Tusser and Fitzherbert, for their concern is not the great manorial estate but the individual farm managed by the owner or tenant with the help of his wife and a few hired servants. The custom of hiring farm servants at Statute Fairs, which continued until the present century and is so graphically described by Hardy in *Far From the Madding Crowd* (1874), is first heard of in the reign of Elizabeth I. The hiring fairs were held for ten days or a fortnight before Martinmas, 11 November, when the rates of wages for the district were given out publicly. The labourers offering themselves for engagement would stand in a row wearing the signs of their trade, a crook or a tuft of wool for a shepherd, a whip for a carter, a straw for a cowman. Many farmhouse inventories mention a servants' chamber, and the regular farmhands also lived in. They were usually the bailiff (on a wealthy farm), the foreman or 'chief hind', the ploughman and the carter, the shepherd and the 'common hind'. In addition to these servants there were the day labourers who were sometimes given meals and whose wages varied according to the season. At the busiest time of the year the farmer also employed 'task workers', who were paid by the acre.

The specialization and innovations attempted by Tudor and Stuart farmers would not have been possible in the open fields. Enclosure was advocated by both Fitzherbert and Tusser:

> The country enclosed I praise,

wrote the latter,

> The other delighteth me not
> For nothing the wealth it doth raise
> To such as inferior be.

and

> More plenty of mutton and beef
> Corn, butter and cheese of the best,
> More wealth anywhere (to be brief)
> More people, more handsome and prest
> Where find ye (go search any coast)
> Than ther, where enclosures are most.

The enclosure of land with permanent hedges for agricultural purposes had been going on throughout the Middle Ages. The landscape towards the west below the Trent and towards the east and south-east was already a patchwork of small hedged fields, scattered farms and meandering lanes. When John Leland (the first of the great Tudor topographers and antiquarians) was travelling between 1534 and 1543 he noticed that much of Devon was hedged by high banks crowned with ash, oak and hazel and that most of Somerset had been enclosed. A decade later, with a growing population, widespread interest in farming methods, and huge tracts of land changing hands after the suppression of the great abbeys, enclosure was proceeding at a faster rate than ever before. It took several forms. First, forest and waste land were enclosed. This was the traditional way of increasing arable and pasture, and a spectacular example of it was the reclamation by the middle of the 17th century of the watery solitudes of the vast fen that stretched from Cambridge to Lincoln and from King's Lynn to Peterborough. Secondly commons were enclosed to prevent haphazard breeding. And thirdly open field strips were transformed into hedged fields, often for grazing, especially in the Midlands. In the process villages and hamlets were sometimes wiped off the face of the earth: in Leicestershire as many as sixty villages had vanished by 1600 and cattle and sheep were feeding on grass which covered the foundations of deserted homesteads.

Both foreign and native travellers in Tudor England stood amazed at the numbers and sizes of the flocks of sheep they saw. Fleeces rather than corn were stored in the great red brick barn at Crows Hall, Debenham (Suffolk), when it belonged to Bassingbourn Gawdy, and a ram's head of moulded brick looks out from the wall to commemorate that usage. According to an act passed in 1534 to limit the number of sheep that might be owned by a single individual, some farmers possessed as many as 24,000 animals. Sheep were the commonest source of wealth and their importance is reflected in the vitality and power of the pastoral theme in the poetry of Spenser, Shakespeare and Herrick and later of Milton. The animals which produced the finest wool, the most valuable in the world, fed on the thin upland pastures which alternate with the clay valleys in the geological structure of the island. They were leaner than the sheep that enjoyed more succulent fields but, owing to some peculiarity of the soil, they grew the best fleeces.

The conversion of arable land to pasture aroused deep resentment. 'Where forty persons had their livings, now one man and his sheep hath all', cried Latimer, preaching against commercial landowners. And in Norfolk Kett and his followers slaughtered 20,000 sheep in 1549 – although enclosure for grazing could scarcely have caused serious hardship in that part of East Anglia where, when the antiquary William Camden visited it in 1586, hardly any open fields had been hedged. No, Kett's violence must have been an instinctive reaction to inevitable change and an understandable protest against the injustice which in some measure was bound to accompany the metamorphosis of the peasant into farmer or landless labourer. It was in the hope of enabling farmworkers to become independent of common and arable land that the famous statute of 1589 ordered that no new cottage was to be built unless it was surrounded by 4 acres of land. Nor was more than one family to occupy a single dwelling. The act was seldom enforced. Records of parishes in north-west Essex and parts of Suffolk in the 16th century disclose that though a cottage plot might be 80 feet square it was not unusual for a plot of half that size to be let; and on several occasions two tenants are named as occupying one cottage, each of them paying the full rent. This situation was not peculiar to Essex and Suffolk, for in his absorbing *History of Myddle*, written towards the end of the 17th century, Richard Gough tells of a cottage in that Shropshire parish which in the early years of Charles I's reign was shared by William Vaughan, a weaver, and Adam Dale, a mason.

The Act speaks of the 'erection of great numbers of cottages which are daily more increased in many parts of this Realme'. The numbers can be imagined when one learns that in the small Lincolnshire parish of Epworth alone one hundred additional cottages were built during the last quarter of the 16th century. The principal reason for so much new building was to provide shelter for the rapidly increasing population. I have already referred to the growth of London; in the country the increase is thought to have been more than fifty per cent in two generations. Domestic building was also affected by the tremendous social changes of the Tudor period. Parish records of progressive areas such as Bedfordshire, Nottinghamshire, Leicestershire and Lincolnshire show that the population was continually changing during the second half of the 16th century. This mobility was accompanied by changes in the relations of the social classes. The nobility were becoming less important; some yeomen farmers were moving into the ranks of the gentry and acquiring manors on which their fathers had been tenants. At the same time the numbers of their own 'middle' class were swelling. Vast traffic in land was going on and houses were everywhere needed on the growing estates of new owners and their tenants.

Richard Gough continually mentions the building of cottages on the commons by forebears of the parishioners of his own day, rural labourers who for the most part had come from other parts of the country. Ellice Hamner had erected a cottage in Myddle Wood in 1581; some time later John Wagge 'inclosed some peices out of Myddle Wood and made it a small tenement'; Evan Jones – 'he couald speake neither good Welsh nor English' – built 'a lytle hutt upon Myddle Wood near the Clay lake, att the higher end of the towne and inclosed a peice out of the Common'. Evan's son William also enclosed land in Myddle Wood and built a cottage.

Countless more substantial farmhouses were also making their appearance on the newly reclaimed wastelands. Among them were the gaunt and forbidding Pit House Farm, afterwards a Cromwellian stronghold, a landmark on the high, inclement expanse of Tow Law, Co. Durham; Pizwell, which grew into a tiny hamlet on the louring slopes of Dartmoor; North Lees Hall, the romantic, towered home of the Eyres on the wild fell above Hathersage in Derbyshire; and Moorhays Farm, near Cruwys Morchard in Devon, where William Zellecke had acquired the lease of a 'parcell of waste ground'. Existing farmhouses were undergoing alteration to provide comforts unknown to their builders; sometimes they were enlarged, sometimes entirely or partially rebuilt in more durable materials, sometimes divided into two or more dwellings. Whole villages of timber-framed dwellings on the limestone belt and in the uplands of Lancashire and the Yorkshire Dales were replaced by stone-built farmsteads and cottages. The spate of building slackened during the Civil War and was slightly interrupted by outbreaks of plague, but its impetus defied all checks, and certainly by the end of the 17th century the numbers of new houses had wrought a greater change in the landscape than the increased extent of hedges and walls.

So extraordinary is the wealth of houses left by the 16th and 17th centuries that thousands still testify to the energetic spirit of that period. The most obviously remarkable of these houses are the great Elizabethan and Jacobean mansions, ostentatious and ebullient, flaunting their strapwork parapets, their pillared porches and their ranges of huge intricately leaded windows from prominent sites. But the farmsteads and cottages of this wonderful age are no less satisfying to the imagination and no less ravishing to the eye. Unsophisticated though they may be they inhabit the same domain of fantasy and high romance as Hardwick and

63

Wollaton. For what image could appear stranger than Houchins, at Feering 68
in Essex, with its grotesquely exaggerated cross-wing, what more
improbable than the heavy black devices on the white walls of Oak Farm, at 65
Styal in Cheshire, what more bewitching and more visionary than the
combination in the fabric of humble Hammoon Manor of Dorset thatch
and a pedimented stone porch lit by a Tudor window and entered between
ringed and swelling Baroque columns? They and their like belong to the
countryside of Shakespeare and still, however altered, evoke the
Shakespearean world of rich pastoral and adumbrate the old rural
certainties.

FARMING AND FARM BUILDINGS

Now, for the first time, no doubt because they were constructed of more
durable materials than in earlier periods, we encounter farmsteads which
include all the familiar structures. Owing to the conservative character of
farm buildings and the continued use for so many centuries of local
materials for their construction it is not easy to date them, but the year of
building or alteration so often proudly recorded on the farmhouse itself –
in the arabic numerals which became popular after the Reformation – may
sometimes give an indication of the age of the adjacent cattle and cart sheds,
granaries and barns.

The two most commonly occurring forms of layout of the farmstead, the
courtyard and the linear, were noted earlier; but 16th- and 17th-century
groups reveal many variations on these two themes. The linear
arrangement remains typical of the north and the south-west. At Blencarn 29
in Cumberland haylofts, cowbyres and stables of coarse dark red sandstone 40
and primitive aspect make a low L-shape about a midden a little distance
from the farmhouse, now called Pleasant View because it overlooks
Dufton Fell. At Redgate Farm, Wolsingham, Co. Durham, the house and 30
outbuildings form a narrow courtyard of sombre masonry pressed down,
under the brow of a hill (or 'wray' as the farmer calls it), by the huge stone
slates which roof the whole farmstead defying winter and tornado winds to
do their worst. At Blentarn, Easedale, a Westmorland farm well known to
Dorothy and William Wordsworth, the hayloft and stable stand parallel
to the long line of the farmhouse and cowbyre, while at Brimmerhead the
little farm buildings are scattered. At Newton, Yorkshire, a pond village
established despite its name before the Conquest, a 19th-century farmhouse
adjoins the long-house it replaced, and a 17th-century barn carries the line
of these buildings beyond a row of structures set at right angles to the long-
house, the whole creating a half-H pattern.

Farms farther south show as much diversity in arrangement. A farmhouse and farm buildings at Clenston, Dorset, make an irregular U
design; farmsteads at Coln Rogers, Gloucestershire, and at Heytesbury, 28
Wiltshire, conform loosely to the quadrangular model; while at Field Farm,
Bibury, in Gloucestershire, the farm buildings stand in line away from the 31
farmhouse, and at Abbess Roding, Essex, the farm buildings, now all 32
sheathed in tarred weatherboarding, are gathered into a courtyard to one
side of the farmhouse.

29 *Right* Long-house, Birk Howe, Little Langdale, Westmorland. The chimneys, plastered and protected by slate ridges, and the sturdy porches are characteristic of the region. The central porch leads into the house, the opening on the right into the animal shelter, of rougher masonry (see p. 89).

30 *Below* Redgate Farm, near Wolsingham, Co. Durham. Dark millstone grit is covered by huge roof slates.

31 *Opposite, above* Barn, granary, hayloft with outshot, and stable at Field Farm, Bibury, Gloucestershire.

32 *Opposite, below* A 16th-century farm at Abbess Roding, Essex. Tarred barns and white houses are a distinctive feature of the Essex landscape.

33 Dovecote, Willington, Bedfordshire.

The barns and dovecotes which are almost the only relics of medieval farming remained conspicuous objects in the steading despite the appearance of other buildings. Pigeon keeping was no longer the monopoly of the lord of the manor: John Norden (whose lifelong endeavour was to make a complete survey of the country shire by shire, the *Speculum Britanniae*) estimated that there were as many as 26,000 dovecotes in England in his day. Nesting boxes for pigeons might be incorporated in the walls and gables of farmhouses and even cottages. They make a band of ornament under the porch eaves of a small farmhouse at Widecombe, Devon; they pattern a cottage gable at Little Rissington, Gloucestershire; dot the front of a porch at Southrop nearby; and spread in three broad tiers across the gable of a farmhouse at Little Milton, Oxfordshire. Dovecotes of the 16th and 17th centuries tend to be square or rectangular rather than circular in shape; they are emphatic products of their region and can on occasion rival the craziest 18th-century folly in the freakish humour of their architecture. The toy-like dovecote at Luntley, Herefordshire, parodies the ponderous stone slating and the bizarre square-panelled black-and-white style of the West Midlands with its miniature scale. Sir John Gostwick's dovecote at Willington, Bedfordshire, built in about 1540 of local limestone rubble and stone from two nearby priories demolished a few years previously, is an eyecatcher with the force of a thunderbolt. It starts up abruptly from an absolutely flat landscape, a preposterously tall narrow rectangle in the form of a fantastic nave and aisles with openings for the pigeons along the clerestory and with stepped gables exaggerating the plunging lines of the roof slopes, not just at either end but in the centre of the roof as well to mark the division between the two nesting chambers within. Tiers of windbraces both support and adorn the trimly carpentered high queen-post roof above the nesting boxes, many hundreds of them, set in the masonry in orderly rows.

The interiors of barns such as those of Parsonage Farm, at Stebbing in Essex, which like others of this period has a single aisle, and the ones at Yelling and St Ives in Huntingdonshire (the latter belonging to the East 36 Midlands Marketing Association and so preserved), strongly recall the barns of the Middle Ages but are distinguished from them by greater severity and economy in the organization of the roof and also, where the building itself is of timber, of the frame. But a thatched, timbered barn at Etchingham in Sussex does give a hint of that sudden leap of the 35 imagination which irradiates so many everyday products of the 16th century. The long cruck-like braces which at Cherhill passed from the base 15 of the wall right across the aisle to support the arcade posts branch out from the centre of the barn floor at Etchingham, sustaining the stout wall plates of the unaisled structure and creating the spectacular visual effect of a great inverted cruck.

The Etchingham barn is unique; but if the Yelling interior – like the 36 majority of 16th- and 17th-century examples – shows no striking constructional developments there is one aspect of this building which is altogether novel: its walls are of brick. Bricks were not made in England after the departure of the Romans until the end of the 13th century, when they were used in the fabric of Little Wenham Hall, Suffolk. Three hundred years went by before a barn was built of brick and the site of it was, significantly, also in East Anglia, partly because of the relative shortage of stone in an area where timber was becoming scarce and partly because of the trading connections of this region with the Netherlands, where brick building had long been established. The vast early 16th-century barn of Hall Farm, at Hales in Norfolk, glows with a colour nearer vermilion than 34 terracotta, varied here and there by a header of cinder hue vitrified in the firing. Bricks depend for their colour on the local clay, which in most of Norfolk contains a high proportion of iron staining it a rich red when fired. The strong colour of this immense barn, the largest in the county, and the outlandish proportions of the stepped gables outlined by mouldings and marked by the crumbling remains of the gablets with which they were once furnished, leave, like the Willington Dovecote, an impression of 33 strangeness and excitement, revealing for a moment the unfamiliar habit of mind which made such a composition possible. A brick barn at Great Gransden, Huntingdonshire, built more than a hundred years later, is by contrast of sober design and subdued rose colour, articulated by the calm rhythm of large regular ventilation slits; while the red madder bricks of a hay barn at Mottram St Andrew, Cheshire, impart a dark intensity to the building. There the simple omission of headers, leaving precise square little openings in the wall, produces an attractive geometric decoration and ventilates the building at the same time.

Tudor and Stuart barns are not usually seen in isolation, as some of their medieval counterparts are, but as part of the farmstead group. All over the country very modest outbuildings can be seen, lean-to shelters for animals, poultry or implements, stables or byres for a single cow or horse, such as those at Brimmerhead in Easedale, the wild valley between Helm Crag and Silver How in Westmorland, and at Widecombe, in a luxuriant declivity in 37 the Devon moors, which differ from each other sharply in setting and fabric

34 *Above* A 16th-century brick barn with Netherlandish crow-stepped gables at Hales, Norfolk.

35 *Left* Barn at Etchingham, Sussex, also of the 16th century.

36 *Below* Interior of the 17th-century brick barn at Church Farm, Yelling, Huntingdonshire.

37 *Above* Widecombe-in-
the-Moor, Devon. On the
left cowbyre and hayloft,
in the foreground a
humble stable, all of
granite, slatestone and
lava – as is the house, in
the background, with a
row of dove-holes below
its porch roof.

38 *Left* Former lodge of
Campden House serving
as a shelter for livestock
at Chipping Campden,
Gloucestershire.

Opposite
VII Brick nogging at
Water Stratford,
Buckinghamshire.
(See p. 111.)

but scarcely at all in form. And many farms include makeshift buildings, like the Nissen huts mentioned at the beginning of this book, or buildings which had another use when they were first erected. Esthwaite Hall in
72 Lancashire sank to the rank of stable and hayloft when it was replaced by a large pretentious mansion in the 19th century, and pigs and livestock took
38 over the ashlared lodges of Sir Baptist Hicks's house at Chipping Campden, Gloucestershire, after it was destroyed in the Civil War.

In general whatever their size farms comprise the same categories of buildings – barn, stable, granary, cowhouse, cart shed and perhaps a piggery. The emphasis, however, differs according to the type of farming the buildings serve. Where arable farming predominates the barn remains the most important and conspicuous structure. In pastoral country, on the other hand, barns are small, and the long two-storeyed range with stable and byre on the ground floor and a hayloft or perhaps a granary above, usually entered by an outside stair, becomes the principal building. In
28 Gloucestershire at Coln Rogers the gigantic barn dwarfs even the
31 farmhouse with its lofty chimneys, and at Field Farm, Bibury, where the linear arrangement of the farm buildings, characteristic of the north rather than of the Cotswolds, has been remarked, the towering proportions of the barn and its gabled door give the group a dramatic accent and totally distinguish it from any assemblage of northern buildings. The line of the
41 farm buildings at Harthill Hall Farm, Alport, Derbyshire, for instance, is powerfully horizontal and it is the massive rectangle of the cowbyre and hayloft which most catches the eye. This building, which incorporates fragments of a 13th-century monastery in its rude masonry, is charged with a wholly unsophisticated air of grandeur which ennobles many northern
40 structures of this kind. The dusky red sandstone ranges at Blencarn, and the gaunt tall cowhouse and hayloft at North Lees Hall Farm, Hathersage, with huge lintels and door jambs like those of a Saxon church, are among innumerable compelling images. Elizabethan and Jacobean farmers thought air and light harmful to the cattle: ventilation was provided only by slit apertures, two of which can still be seen at Hathersage, while at Blencarn they survive unaltered. Windows were inserted in the upper floor if grain was kept there, and the great first-floor storage rooms at both Hathersage and Alport are lit; at Hathersage the room is warmed by a wall fireplace. Chimneys can often be seen rising from granaries: there is one at Coln Rogers and another at Fenstead End, Suffolk. The grain was usually kept in chests (called 'kists' in the north) or in bins.

The ground-floor doors at Blencarn open into manure passages and drains. The cows are tethered noses towards their mangers and tails towards the manure passage. At Hathersage the arrangement was the same before the doors were blocked. The internal arrangement can be seen in the
44 byre at Courthouse Farm, Hawkshead, Lancashire. Another plan is
43 memorably embodied in the byre of Haddon Field Farm, Alport, Derbyshire, where the cows are stalled along instead of across the building, between shaped partitions, and in the shadow of a crushingly powerful king-post roof, a type of structure common in northern farm buildings of the 16th and 17th centuries. When the byre was built the stalls were yet more confined, for the roof then contained a loft.

At Cowmire Hall, Cartmel Fell, Lancashire, which bears a late 17th-century date, the hayloft and cowbyre conform to the design which emerged in Tudor times but they are articulated in a way which is peculiar to regions with a heavy rainfall. The joists of the hayloft floor project as for a jetty and support an inclined stone-slated roof, a welcome shelter for the labourer cleaning out the manure passages. The marked accent of this horizontal feature draws the eye to the abrupt and interesting contrast between the height, colour and texture of the walls of the hayloft and those of the byre below. The picturesque fabric of the upper storey, dry-stone walling tufted with bright yellow, long-haired bog moss, is intensified by the whitewash of the squat cowhouse to which, as at Blencarn, light is admitted through the tiniest openings, known locally as 'lap-oils'. At Brimmerhead, a stable with a hayloft above it shows the same projecting feature. One of the windows is original – for while early cowstalls were always low and dark, horses were given taller, better-lit quarters. The round opening at the top of the gable seems to indicate that the classical form of this nobly proportioned little building, which would not look out of place in the Tuscan hills, was intentional, but this is not so: such circular openings were traditional and were known as 'pitching eyes'. From them hay was flung to animals in the yard outside.

In the Lake District the projection often supported an open gallery in the 16th and 17th centuries, though such galleries were already becoming rare when De Quincey observed them during his visits to the Wordsworths between 1807 and 1809 and remarked that they were a peculiarity of the region. Only five examples were listed by Professor Barley in 1961, though his list did not include the gallery at Yew Tree Farm, Coniston, Lancashire. It rests on tremendous joists, open for most of its rugged length but filled with wattle-and-daub panels where it joins the farmhouse and roofed with huge mossy stone slates. Another unassuming little gallery juts from an

39 Gallery at Yew Tree Farm, Coniston, Lancashire.

42

40

46

Opposite
VIII Limestone (including two blocks of ironstone) at Stanion, Northamptonshire. Geraniums screen the inhabitants within.

40 *Above* Foldyard and midden at Blencarn, Cumberland.

41, 42 *Below and right* Cowbyres with haylofts at Harthill Hall Farm, Alport, Derbyshire, and Cowmire Hall, Cartmel Fell, Lancashire.

43, 44 *Opposite* Cowbyres at Haddon Field Farm, Alport, Derbyshire, and Courthouse Farm, Hawkshead, Lancashire.

outhouse at Hawkshead, approached by uneven rock-like steps which lead also into the hayloft alongside the gallery. Such roofed projections are thought to be spinning galleries, and may well be, for they usually face north where the light is good and at the time of their origin all the dalesmen's garments were spun and woven at home.

Dual-purpose farm buildings took other forms than the two-storeyed range. In northern pastoral country where little corn was grown the insignificant barn was often combined with a cattleshed under the same roof. And because the building generally stood in undulating, mountainous country it was ingeniously adapted to the terrain. A bank or slope suggested a building on two levels. Such a structure buttressed by lean-tos for pigs and poultry confronts a farmhouse at Lowthwaite in Cumberland from a high bank. A grass-grown ramp leads up to the door of the threshing barn, which faces a much smaller opening high up in the wall on the farmyard side and provides a draught for winnowing. The lower level of the building is entered directly from the farmyard so that the two or three cows it shelters can be easily exercised and watered.

Another dual-purpose building common in the north is the isolated field house, providing food and shelter for cattle and reducing labour in inclement weather and at harvest time. A typical field house affording occasional accommodation for cows at the lower level and with storage for hay at the upper end, fashioned of the pale magnesian limestone beneath it, stands near Hawkswick in Yorkshire. The lonely building is both a manifestation and an extension of the landscape, the quiet meadows going down to the Skirwith river and the immense solitary sweep of rock on the far side of the water, soon to become the precipice of Malham.

It may seem surprising to find large barns in regions such as the Cotswolds which derived so much wealth from sheep farming, but they testify to the practice of mixed farming which though varying in proportion was characteristic of traditional husbandry. Norden, travelling through Gloucestershire in 1620, admired 'the fertile corne grounde and lardge Fields greatly inriching the industrious Husbandman'. Such barns were already occasionally being used, as they would be later, for housing

47

45

45 *Right* An isolated field house built on two levels near Hawkswick, Yorkshire.

46 *Opposite, above* Stable and hayloft at Brimmerhead, Easedale, Westmorland. The rough masonry – slatestone, granite and random lumps of lava – is only lightly set with mortar.

47 *Opposite, below* A bank barn at St John's Vale, Lowthwaite, Cumberland. A building on two levels adapted to the sloping terrain and comprising a barn and animal shelter with lean-tos for pigs and poultry.

49 cattle. The barn of Old Hall Farm, Woodford, Cheshire, dated 1660, was built with a hayloft and cowhouse at one end. Subsidiary farm buildings were often attached to large barns. At Siddington in Gloucestershire, where the broad-aisled 16th-century building is so akin in shape and texture to the adjacent church; at Aldworth in Berkshire, with its enormous porch of ecclesiastic design pierced by cruciform openings and lit by a narrow glazed window beneath a sundial; in Gloucestershire, at Village Farm,

48 Winson, and at Ablington, where two barns, one of the early 18th century, the other a gigantic Elizabethan building, stand side by side – at all these places shelter sheds have been built under the extended roof of the barn, alongside the projecting porch.

These open-fronted shelters, where cattle could take refuge from the weather at their will, are often found in parts of the country where dairy cows were not housed for the winter in stalls. If they are not built against the barn they are often attached to the wall of the foldyard, and in the 17th century even these humble structures could achieve distinction, so exquisitely were they attuned to their setting. A remarkable pillared building near Coln St Aldwyns, Gloucestershire, deploys its weathered shafts and capitals of finest stone with the gesture of a grand classical colonnade. The farm stands on Akeman Street close to the site of a Roman villa, and it was from there, according to tradition, that the columns came.

48 Fine Cotswold barns at Ablington, Gloucestershire, with subsidiary farm buildings attached to them. In the porch is Michael À Bere, descendant of the original tenant.

Cart sheds as well as cow shelters were built with open fronts; and there are references to such sheds in the literature of the period. In his *Rural Economy of Yorkshire in 1641* Henry Best boasts of his seven carts kept in two sheds. It was not uncommon for the cart shed to occupy the open-fronted ground floor of a granary, as it does at Washford, Somerset, where the building is of red sandstone rubble and was once thatched.

Freestanding granaries used only for the storage of grain, found in corn-growing regions, are raised from the ground to keep out thieving rats. The shaped stones sometimes used for this purpose, called staddle stones, have now often become giant mushrooms in suburban gardens. The miniature proportions of a square granary at Arrington, Cambridgeshire, with a pyramidal roof topped by a rudimentary ball finial, seem to point to a low grain yield, though probably at the time when the building was erected the grain was kept for village consumption only.

FARMHOUSES AND COTTAGES

The distinction between farmhouses of the great centuries of vernacular building and what we now call cottages is far from clear. In the north the surviving 16th- or 17th-century 'cottage' was nearly always built as a farmstead and often still serves that purpose. The homes labourers built for themselves on the new enclosures were, according to contemporary accounts, the most wretched, unsubstantial hovels. Gough tells of a one-legged man who lived in a cave, though 'Bickley alias Hall' was not quite respectable: he was more often maintained by the parish than by his own work and was probably not married to the mother of his three children. 'He *says* shee is his wife', remarks Gough. Thomas Chidlow of Myddle lived in

49 *Above left* Barn of Old Hall Farm, Woodford, Cheshire, dated 1660, partly adapted as a cowbyre and hayloft with open timber front.

50 *Above* Open-fronted shelter of fine architectural character on Akeman Street, near Coln St Aldwyns, Gloucestershire.

81

'a poore pitifull hut, built up to an old oake'. Richard Carew, in his *Survey of Cornwall* written in 1580–90, describes cottages 'in times not past the remembrance of some yet living' built of rammed earth with 'low thatched roofs, few partitions, no planchings or glasse windows, and scarcely any chimnies other than a hole in the wall to let out the smoke'. The character of two cottages on the manor of Glupton in Oxfordshire can be imagined from the information given in an inventory that they were valued at £3 for the pair in 1631: each consisted of but one room. Any dwellings of this kind which may survive must be among those which were later improved; and there is evidence that alterations were occasionally made. Gough mentions several cottages which were enlarged by the addition of another bay or by the insertion of a chimney and an attic floor: Anne Chidley lived in 'a lyttle house in Newton that had noe chimney' but the next tenant, Richard Clarke, built a chimney. Daniel King, the Cheshire topographer, also writes of cottagers who 'builded chimnies and furnished other parts of their houses accordingly'.

Village streets usually show a little house here and there that looks as though it might have started life as a one- or two-roomed dwelling. A cottage at Dorchester in Oxfordshire may, like Anne Chidley's, have become two-floored with the later introduction of a chimney and a loft, for that is what is indicated by the partial withdrawal of the thatch from the picturesque roof to make room for tiles and a dormer window. But many cottages have been made by dividing former hall-house farms like those mentioned in the last chapter, and numbers of pairs of cottages have been contrived from the rectangular derivatives of the hall-house.

Pairs of cottages built from the latter half of the 17th century onwards were, however, frequently designed specially for rural labourers and their families. Two such little dwellings, thatched and of sandstone, shelter in an obscurity of myrtles below a rocky incline at Buckland-in-the-Moor,

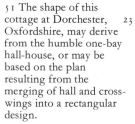

51 The shape of this cottage at Dorchester, 23 Oxfordshire, may derive from the humble one-bay hall-house, or may be based on the plan resulting from the merging of hall and cross-wings into a rectangular design.

52 An early instance
(17th-century) of a terrace
of one-storeyed dwellings
built of brick and
originally thatched, at
Tattershall, Lincolnshire.

Devon: the chimneys are incorporated in the gable ends and the doors are symmetrically placed. The like of such cottages can be seen in most villages, always with the differences conferred by locality. Occasionally a row of cottages survives from the 17th century. The famous example in Gloucestershire at Arlington, Bibury, a single steep roof of stone tiles interrupted by irregular gables and dormers above oddly placed doors, was built to house weavers making cloth for fulling at Arlington Mill. A contrasting row carried out in clunch and thatch sweeps smoothly along the curve of the street at Melbourn, Cambridgeshire, while at Tattershall in 52 Lincolnshire one-storeyed cottages of brick stretch towards the church under a common roof, each little house containing two rooms. The ridges at the bases of the chimneys show that the roofs were once thatched.

All the delight, all the significance of these little houses lies in their diversity, in the informality of their haphazard compositions so often exaggerated by a huddle of lean-tos, outshots and projections, in the unsophisticated craftsmanship which has given each one of them its own singularity, above all in the way they are absorbed into the landscape, settling into it as naturally as a yellowhammer's nest into a hedgebank. To talk of anything like a deliberate plan seems absurdly out of place. Yet

53 At Westbury Farm, Ashwell, Hertfordshire, the jettied wings and hall block are still distinct. The higher roof level of the hall block shows that it was raised to give headroom when an upper floor was introduced.

traditional arrangements have shaped the cottages so far described and when we turn to the dwellings we now call cottages, but which were originally the homes of husbandmen, that tradition becomes more strongly evident.

Confirmation of the sense that these houses were not built as cottages comes from the thousands of inventories of the 16th and 17th centuries of goods taken for probate, for many of them name the rooms in which the objects were found and give a clear picture of the layout of the structure. Again and again the records refer to very small houses consisting of but a hall, sometimes called 'the house', a term still heard in the north, and a parlour with a kitchen which may be an outshot at the opposite end. Robert Smalley of Galby in Leicestershire, who died in 1559, and George Clinch of Bletchingley in Surrey, who died in the first quarter of the 17th century, though separated in time by more than fifty years, lived in identical houses of this kind with a loft over the hall and parlour. They both owned several cows, pigs and a team of horses, so they were more than labourers. Another small farmhouse in the parish of Bletchingley, belonging to John Crackett who was Robert Smalley's contemporary, showed the same plan but had chambers instead of lofts above the parlour and kitchen. Similar farmsteads are chronicled for Berkshire, Yorkshire, Sussex, Kent, Buckinghamshire, Suffolk and Essex and it is probably true to say that where they still stand V they have become the cottages we know today.

The majority of larger farmhouses appear to have contained six to eight rooms. Thus William Laken of Elmsall in Yorkshire, who in 1563 was living in the farmhouse which a little later was rebuilt by Henry Best's grandfather, had three parlours, one of which was for his servants, and three chambers. Richard Wolfe of Roxwell, Essex, who owned a large farm and grew hops towards the end of the 17th century, had a hall, two parlours, a little closet, a kitchen, two butteries, a brewhouse, a milkhouse and a boulting house (where flour was 'bolted' or sifted to separate it from the bran); on the upper floor there were three chambers and a servants' chamber, and above that an attic where oats were stored. Henry Sharke of Writtle in Essex, who died in 1638, had a hall, parlour, great and little buttery, kitchen and milkhouse, and a servants' chamber and other chambers over parlour and hall. William Boosey, who was farming in the same parish nearly fifty years later, owned a house with exactly the same accommodation.

House design in this period was dominated by the trend, noticeable already in the later Middle Ages, towards the achievement of a compact two-storeyed form. The stages by which this came about can be observed and described, but the changes were attended by every conceivable variation that high-spirited craftsmen and owners could devise and the metamorphosis outlined here is necessarily a great simplification.

In numbers of early 16th-century houses, the hall block and cross-wings remain distinct although the house is two-storeyed throughout. The hall block, because it now has two floors, rises above the cross-wings and these are further differentiated by their jetties. The cross-wings of 17th-century houses are generally neither jettied nor projecting: they have become gables rising at either end of a flat façade, as at Abbey Farm, Hacheston,

54 At Abbey Farm, Hacheston, Suffolk, the cross-wings, brought entirely into line with the hall block, are marked only by their gables.

55 A thatched attempt to
achieve a continuous roof
line at Fuller's End,
Elsenham, Essex.

56 At Office Farm,
Methwold, Norfolk,
even the gables have
disappeared. The house
has become completely
rectangular and only the
position of door and
chimney recall the hall-
house design.

Suffolk. The tradition of the cross-wings does however persist at the rear of Abbey Farm, where one wing advances slightly and a whole block comes forward from the other. This is a common feature: it was the 'backhouse' containing the dairy and perhaps the brewery. In the final stage of the emerging rectangular plan the gables disappear. In some instances the jetty may persist and continue all round the house, but more often the composition is a plain oblong. This form of farmhouse appears in many guises: it manifests itself in plastered half-timber at Methwold, Norfolk, in plastered clunch at Ashton Keynes, Wiltshire, in square-panelled black and white half-timber near Clifton-on-Teme, Worcestershire, grandly in brick and half-timber at Flemings Hall, Bedingfield, Suffolk, in stone and half-timber at Gardiners Farm, Aston Subedge, Gloucestershire, and in sandstone and thatch in the lonely, humble little farm of Higher Pudnes, near Buckland in Devon. These are but random instances of countless versions of the theme.

When old houses were altered to conform to the fashionable rectangular shape the results could be visually odd. The consequences of enthusiasm for the oblong shape in a farmhouse at Fuller's End, Essex, are entrancingly grotesque. The half-timbered house consists of the traditional hall, once one-storeyed but with a loft and dormer inserted later, and separately roofed cross-wings. Either at the time the hall was converted or later still the whole extent of the roof, cross-wings and all, was smothered in thatch in an attempt to unify the structure. Just as a square teacosy on a round pot fails to disguise the bulging rotund form beneath it, so the thatch at Fuller's End, while it presents the unbroken ridge of a rectangular house, leaves the hall-house design fully exposed below: the eaves line is wildly interrupted and the original roofs of the cross-wings can be glimpsed under the thick straw covering.

In these two-storeyed rectangular houses the former screens passage has become an entrance hall, often a through passage as at Newbourn Hall, Suffolk and at Pattenden in Kent, where the hall was ceiled and a chimney inserted in about 1530. In modest farmhouses there is often, however, no vestibule and the traditional screens passage is remembered only by the position of the door which opens straight into the principal room (sometimes, recalling the hall from which it derived, known as the 'fire-room'). A cottage at Great Leighs, Essex, built as a farmhouse at the end of the 16th century, still exhibits the characteristic arrangement. The door, placed according to custom near the kitchen end of the house, leads directly into the living room, and a small parlour opens from the upper end of this room.

There are four attic rooms at Great Leighs and it is apparent from an opening in the floor over the parlour that access to two of them was by a ladder from this room. There is no door between these two upper rooms and the remaining two; these last were entered by means of a ladder set against the outer wall of the kitchen. They were no doubt used for storage, as they were in a similar house at Pulborough, Sussex, where a 16th-century owner, Henry Miles, kept yarn, hemp and wool in the loft over the kitchen and part of the hall.

The present staircases at Great Leighs must have replaced the ladders some time after the end of the 17th century, for it was only then that stairs were constructed of boards for separate treads and risers. The wooden staircases which first replaced ladders consisted of solid blocks of oak and were of the newel design, like the winding stair in North Lees Hall Farm at Hathersage; or the quarter-newel design starting off as a straight flight, then turning up to the first floor, as at Crows Hall, Debenham; or of the

57
26

57 *Below left* Newbourn Hall, Suffolk: the entrance hall which evolved from the screens passage.

58 *Below* The steps of the staircase at Crows Hall, Debenham, Suffolk, are constructed of solid timbers and ascend in two short, straight flights. The turned balusters were a 17th-century addition.

59–61 Cheery Nook, Matterdale, Cumberland. *Above*, the long-house, the animal shelter of which was at the end nearest the camera. The inclined slates on the squat chimney prevent down-draughts. *Below*, the 'house-place' or living room, showing the traditional fitted cupboards against the cross-passage, and Mr and Mrs Abbott seated at the other end of the room by the kitchen range and glazed stoneware sink (see p. 197).

dog-legged type ascending in two straight flights, the second returning in the opposite direction to that of the first. Such staircases might be accommodated in a rounded or rectangular projection; more often they were placed in the hall, sometimes set against an internal chimneystack as at Office Farm, Methwold.

In the highland region a change was taking place in the plan of the long-house, bringing it closer to that of the two-storeyed farmhouse with or without a through passage. In the Lake District at Birk Howe the cows still share the farmer's roof but not his door. The door into the house is now separated from the cross passage by a little kitchen and there is no access to the house from the passage. Fellfoot Farm, grander in scale than most Lake District farmsteads and romantically sited below a frowning crag at the foot of Wrynose Pass, displays another modification of the long-house structure: the cowbyre and hayloft are separately roofed and are placed at the upper end of the farmhouse rather than at the service end, an arrangement which became increasingly common from the second half of the 17th century.

Sometimes, as at Cheery Nook Farm, Matterdale, the cross passage (or 'hallen' to give it the local name by which it now became known), divided from the cowhouse by a stone wall and entered by the broad, rugged porch characteristic of mountain cottages, is part of the living room but is separated from it by a screen of built-in cupboards – the 'heck' – with a door in the middle. This feature is instantly reminiscent of the medieval screen, though it seems only to have become customary in the Lake District

62 At Fellfoot Farm, Wrynose Pass, Westmorland, the house stands in line with its farm buildings but is not a true long-house because the structures are separately roofed and there is no communication between them.

29
62

59

60

89

in the early 17th century. The affinity with the screens passage is especially

p.1 striking if one stands in the passage of a farmhouse such as Underhowe, Grasmere, with the door between the cupboards open: it is at once obvious that they are a partition in a single apartment. In later houses where an actual wall divides passage and living room the traditional cupboards are still set against it, as at Wallthwaite Farm, Great Langdale. These cupboards of dark, highly polished oak, panelled and carved, usually bear the initials of the owner and the date. The cupboards at Matterdale are dated 1631 and those at Wallthwaite Farm 1711.

The development of farm buildings, farmhouses and cottages, even when like these Lakeland homes their wildness and kinship with the naked rock direct the thoughts to poetry rather than planning, depended on basic needs, and even ornamental features such as the fitted cupboards I have just

46 described or the roundel in the hayloft gable at Brimmerhead might be adopted in the first place for practical reasons. But in an age of such intense gusto, so ardently in love with the everyday business of living, it was not likely that the aspect of even such modest buildings as farmhouses should be wholly dictated by the incidents of utilitarian construction. A stronger urge too than the desire to conform to the latest fashion lay behind the lively appearance of so many farmhouses. The plain rectangle was an inadequate outlet for the sense of romance, the audacious fantasy, the passionate interest in the past which determined the climate of the period and influenced the taste of the yeoman farmer and the country craftsman as much as of the owners and builders of great mansions.

The tower which so captivated the imagination of Elizabethan magnates and their architects, embodying at the same time their glamorous view of the Middle Ages and their desire for self-advertisement, was not at that time necessary for defence, except in Border country, and it could not be put to essential use on the farm. Nevertheless it was occasionally incorporated in the farmhouse design. Something of the high romance of

63 the Bolsover keep informs the broad towers of North Lees Hall Farm at Hathersage, with their semicircular niched battlements and mullioned windows; neglect and the rudeness of the masonry quicken the romance and the make-believe fortress atmosphere. The rectangular hall block is itself like a tower with the actual tower containing a projecting staircase turret rising only a little above it. The date 1596 is carved in the stained and shabby plasterwork of a handsome, derelict room in the tower, where when I last saw it hens were roosting on a worm-eaten four-poster. At Boothby Graffoe, Lincolnshire, a tall rectangular house was set alongside a fragment of the curtain wall and the circular tower of Somerton Castle. The business of the farm, which is much in evidence here, the white-painted windows, the association of stone with a red brick buttress and warm red tiles, a door painted ginger grown and grained and a pretty Victorian railing weaken what must once have been the ostentatiously chivalric architecture of this conversion. But the tower still rises sharply from a densely overgrown moat and the building still commands the atmospheric view over mournful flats seen by King John of France when he was imprisoned in this very tower after his defeat at Poitiers.

The conspicuous angles and vertical thrust of gables and gablets and the

63 North Lees Hall, Hathersage, Derbyshire, an arresting late 16th-century version of the tower house carried out in rude carboniferous limestone. It was the home of the Eyres, and a descendant of this once powerful Catholic family was farming here in the 1950s.

strong chiaroscuro of boldly advancing wings and storeyed porches, all of which were present in the traditional hall-house, haunted the imagination of Tudor and Stuart builders. The old hall-house plan might still be preferred to newfangled designs: Manor Farm, at Lower Winchendon in Buckinghamshire, was built as late as 1620 with a one-storeyed hall and a cross-wing and a tall porch, though the roof line is continuous. Even when the house was two-storeyed throughout the hall-house plan with a central block and cross-wings might form the basis of an inspired composition and a delectably idiosyncratic interpretation of new motifs. So at Snitterton, Derbyshire, the exterior of Hall Farm takes the familiar form of a central block with cross-wings and an asymmetrically placed door. But the façade between the gables is crenellated, while the gables themselves are adorned with ball-topped finials and the door is surprisingly flanked by thin columns on high bases, a rural mason's eccentric version of the Ionic order, combined with a carved frieze of naturalistic flowers.

A spectacularly gabled variation on the hall-house design catches the eye
64 at Weobley, Herefordshire. Ley Farm is an expressive example of the small-panelled timber style of the region and this encourages the effect of the proliferating gables. From each gabled cross-wing a further two-storeyed gabled projection starts forward. The tall, storeyed porch is surmounted by a gable which jostles the central gable over the bay windows of the hall and the room above it, while above them both yet another purely decorative gable emerges from the slope of the roof.

The hall-house plan with a single cross-wing was much favoured. At
66 Broadoaks in the parish of Wimbish, Essex, the design is clothed in russet-coloured brick, a romantic image, buttressed, yet with a classical roundel in its high gable, bedizened with a display of tall, slim octagonal chimney shafts with bulging caps of prickly spines in two rows: set in groups of two and three on rectangular plinths and broached, moulded bases, they rise from the junction of hall block and cross-wing and from the centre and rear of the hall block itself. As one looks, the whole structure, because the gable is not quite symmetrical, seems slightly to sway on its moated plot, an impression strengthened by the tautly patterned fabric of the building, the fine weave of the small bricks and the glinting criss-cross of the leaded glazing of the large windows whose worn mullions and transoms are moulded in pale terracotta, the Italian material introduced into England some forty years before Broadoaks was built and still fashionable.

65 Hall and cross-wing make the same shape at Styal, Cheshire in the half-timbered house of Oak Farm, but the mood and emphasis could not be more disparate. Whereas the harmonious fabric of Broadoaks is all of a piece, Oak Farm is stone-slated with brick chimneys above half-timbered walls. Whereas Broadoaks tremblingly aspires, Oak Farm is earthbound: the tall chimneys, diagonally set shafts on high plinths, shoot aloft independently, giving no upward impetus to the building as a whole and without power to draw the eye from the drama of the staring black timbers coarsely patterning the white walls with a verve beside which the squares
64 and rectangles of Ley Farm seem to speak in monotones. But it is not just its flamboyance which makes Oak Farm unforgettable, it is above all the carpenter's free, bold allusion to tradition in the decorative use of mighty crucks in the gable end.

The combination of hall and cross-wing was here and there yet more overwhelmingly transfigured by the builder's eager, imaginative grasp of
67 possibilities. At Parsonage Farm, Burwell, Cambridgeshire, the cross-wing, of towering height, brandishes twin gables on the façade of the house and at the rear slopes precipitously down to within a few feet of the ground in the form of an outshot backhouse. The 16th-century builder of Moat Hall, at Parham in Suffolk (where an older house, the seat of the Uffords and Willoughbys, had stood), concentrated all the important living rooms – all the splendour of the house – in the cross-wing. Thus when the house became a farm, after the sole heiress, Catherine Willoughby, married Richard Bertie, of Berstead in Kent, the hall block became the backhouse where the work of the farmhouse was done. The hall block is half-timbered, the cross-wing of fashionable brick now faded, spectral and poignantly beautiful in decay. Its lack of symmetry must always have been

64 Ley Farm, Weobley, Herefordshire, dated 1589, framed in small panels with a profusion of gables.

65 *Above* Oak Farm, Styal, Cheshire, a timber-framed hall-house with a single cross-wing.

66 *Left* At Broadoaks, Wimbish, Essex (*c.* 1560), the hall-house plan with a single cross-wing is carried out in brick.

67 Parsonage Farm, Burwell, Cambridgeshire. The single cross-wing is twin-gabled. The house and outbuildings are of local clunch and chalk lump.

68 At Houchins, Feering, near Coggeshall in Essex, the single cross-wing, three-storeyed and jettied, was added about 1600 to an earlier house and dominates the building. The attic storey was originally lit by small unglazed windows under the eaves.

entrancing. Two mouldering gabled bays with cusped arched lights now half blocked with wattle and daub, and a chimneystack adorned with arcading and, like the bays, with diaper work, project from the corroded walls into the dark moat, thick with weeds, that still encompasses the house.

The cross-wing is similarly exalted above the earlier hall at Houchins, and there takes the form of a huge, toppling house of three jettied storeys. The top floor was used for storage, probably of cloth produced in the area which was famed for its wool industry. (Houchins must have been the centre of arable as well as sheep farming, for the surrounding fields extend to almost 400 acres and an aisled barn of eleven bays is the most prominent of the farm buildings contemporary with the house.) There were two large rooms on both the first and ground floors, and the house was entered, as it still is, by a central door immediately in front of the chimney, which, set into a timber-framed bay, was a bold feature of the architectural design. The dragon beams of the jetties are supported by the swelling, polished carvings of sirens, not the fish-tailed beings of medieval lore but the bird-footed winged creatures of classical mythology. Exactly such fabulous images, according to the illustration in *Arches of Triumph* published in 1604, figured boldly in the spandrels of the arch erected to celebrate James I's entry into London earlier in the same year, and the builder of Houchins, perhaps Thomas Howchynge, who was baptized in 1569, might have seen both the book and the arch itself. The same image appears on either side of the porch of a cottage, once a farmstead, at Weobley. The siren was but one of countless motifs raised from the grave of the distant past by the magic of scholarship to become new sources of inspiration in every sphere and to merge with traditional forms in electrifying synthesis.

Where the flat-fronted style was adopted, gables frequently galvanized the sober rectangular façade into upward movement, departing from the position they had traditionally occupied at the extreme ends of the house. The space between the gables was often so reduced, as at Charendon Farm, Preston Bagot, Warwickshire, that only the placing of the door discloses the hall-house origin of the plan. In the Cotswolds the gables were usually moved still closer together and a little away from the ends of the house, as at Barrington Farm, Great Barrington, and at times they become no more than dormers, considerably lower than the roof ridge.

90

Endymion Porter's rambling rectangular house at Aston Subedge, a rebuilding in stone of an earlier house, includes part of the old half-timbered manor, the panels now filled with stone. A tall ball-crowned gable marks the entrance and immediately beside it rises a twin gable giving a sudden unexpected flicker of movement to the façade, reinforcing the momentum of the tall chimneys and the picturesque irregularity of the long low farmhouse in its wooded hollow. 69

A widely popular design was the triple-gabled façade in which a third gable was set between the two derivations of the cross-wings. The gables on a farmhouse at Finstock, Oxfordshire, enliven the flat front with a quick, 70 sharp ascending and descending rhythm. Oval windows surmounted by dripstones look out from the ball-topped gables and are flanked by ball-topped finials; below them three square-headed mullioned, leaded windows with dripstone mouldings rise above the broader mullioned windows and the door of the ground floor. Already aspiring, the house is drawn yet more impetuously upwards by its tall, finely moulded chimneys. This improbable and felicitous assemblage of incongruous motifs is a typical product of the early 17th century and of limestone country, especially the Cotswolds.

The composition with contiguous gables assumes different forms and expresses other moods elsewhere. At Manor Farm, Toseland, Huntingdon- 71 shire, brick takes the place of the pale stone of Finstock and imparts fiery colour to a riveting image. The design is, for a modest house of 1600, obsessively and untraditionally symmetrical, with projecting bays beneath each of the three gables, a central porch and buttresses at either end of the house and between the bays. Only a small unpaired window on one side of

69 Farmhouse, granary and stable at Aston Subedge, Gloucestershire.

the porch indicates the persistence inside of a hall-house-based plan. A band of billet ornament in moulded brick defines the edges of the upstanding gables and leads the eye toward the preposterous outcrop of chimneys, brick columns with battlemented capitals outlined against the sky in flurries of two and three like gatherings of chess-set castles.

A vital feature of all the two-storeyed houses mentioned here was the chimney: the introduction of the chimney meant that the hall need no longer be open to the roof. The new chimneystacks might taper up at the gable ends of a house, or at the front or back. In the second half of the 17th century chimneys at the gable end were incorporated in the walls. But more often the stack rose through the heart of the house, built between the hall and the service end where there was no screens passage, as at Office Farm, Methwold, or set against the screens passage in grander farmhouses such as Pattenden at Goudhurst and Church Farm at Stebbing.

Where fireplaces had existed in medieval houses they had always been set against an outer wall, and the creative idea of building the stack in the centre of the house was quite as remarkable as the invention of the jetty. When it was added to a house already standing the structural problems, not to speak of the disarray in the lives of the inmates, must have been formidable. But the internal stack had practical advantages: it could service two back-to-back fireplaces on each floor and it gave additional strength to the whole structure. The traditional position of the open hearth may perhaps have suggested the internal stack, and indeed at Tiptofts, Wimbish, the chimney rises on the very spot where the fire burned – and with fantastic pictorial effect, for the hall has not been made into two floors and the great brick intruder fills the upper bay of the room with startling impact on its proportions: its height has become tower-like.

70, 71 Triple-gabled façades at Finstock, Oxfordshire (left) and at Manor Farm, Toseland, Huntingdonshire (c. 1600).

Chimneys vary in design according to the nature of their fabric and their site. Those of farmhouses on the limestone belt, even of the most unassuming character, are of stone, generally square and sometimes set diagonally on a square plinth, their height counterbalanced by one or two reticent horizontal mouldings. In the hills of north Devon and the mountains of the Lake District tall cylinders of irregular stone or of rubble plastered over facilitate the escape of smoke in a sheltered, overhung setting; downdraughts are controlled by two pieces of slate inclined against one another. Such chimneys are strange enough objects, but it was the new material, brick, which prompted the builder's most stupendous inventions and he used it widely, even occasionally where good stone was available. Chimneys were meant to draw the eye and to advertise the important fact that the house had fireplaces. Like the jetty, the chimney became a status symbol, and the number of shafts by no means always corresponded to the number of fireplaces.

To conceive of chimneys as aerial columns with bases, shafts and capitals of wild variety, clustered or single, was to do far more than proclaim a hearth: it was an invention of genius, as much a reflection of the high poetic excitement of the age as the richly polyphonic Elizabethan madrigal and just such another exotic hybrid. A number of these astounding compositions, those at Broadoaks and those at Toseland in particular, have 66,71 already been pointed out, but their diversity and liveliness are endless. The chimneys at Flemings, Bedingfield, are in the form of four octagonal shafts set on high plinths with moulded bases and capitals and with a band of carved ornament, tiny panels filled with rosettes, round the tops. At Houchins a chimney of gargantuan proportions with a huge base and no 68 less than twelve shafts sits darkly on the immensely tall cross-wing,

72 *Above left* A cylindrical Lakeland chimney at Esthwaite, Lancashire, on a building which was once the hall and has now become a stable and hayloft.

73 *Above* An ostentatious and ornate brick chimney at Newport, Essex, with four moulded brick shafts.

74 The ceiling and fireplace inserted into the former open hall of Pattenden Manor, Goudhurst, Kent, in the early 16th century. The magnificent moulding of the beams and lintel was executed with a simple chisel and gouge.

73 pressing it down. A group of four shafts with similar spiny, scalloped and corbelled tops soars with a magnificent flourish from a high, panelled plinth on the roof of a very modest house in the village street at Newport, Essex. But here the shafts are shorter and entirely overlaid with the most intricate designs superbly carried out in carved and moulded brick, a minute mesh of Saracenic character, a banded pattern of linked hexagons and another of loose, lacy openwork. The groups of lofty columns with oversailing capitals that shoot up so surprisingly from the calm white rectangle of a farm at Brent Pelham, Hertfordshire, are neither Gothic nor classic, and the reticulations, diapers, twists and spirals with which they are encrusted give a keener edge to the strangeness of their proportions. The shafts of the massive chimney sitting between hall block and cross-wing
82 at Church Farm, Stebbing, combine in a single ponderous square mass adorned with sharp, angular fluting like crisp pleats, and it rests on a square base with stepped gablets at each corner.

The fireplace whose presence the chimney published from the housetop might be of stone in a stone region but was more often of brick, crowned at the opening with a huge beam of oak, which in more important
74 farmhouses, such as Pattenden, might be carved or moulded. The back of the beam was canted to encourage a draught up the chimney. There was often a corner seat within the fireplace with a little niche near it where the occupant could place a glass or a cup. Iron plates protected the backs of hearths and in the districts of iron foundries – Sussex, Surrey and Kent – the fireback became the medium for robust relief work, figurative and heraldic, much like 17th-century tombstone carving in both form and feeling. The same bold treatment, the same unerring sense for strong, comely shape distinguishes all the other many appurtenances of the hearth which survive from the period: firedogs, an occasional long-handled fire shovel, tongs, roasting spits, chimney cranes, gridirons and pothangers, skillets, cauldrons, pipkins, pans and earthen pots.

Fireplaces in chambers became common in the 17th century. They were narrower than those in the 'hall' or kitchen and might be surmounted by a carving in wood or stone or by plasterwork.

Inventories reveal that the contents of larger farmhouses did not differ greatly except in quantity from those of the homes of husbandmen as humble as Robert Smalley (p. 84). Practically every house was furnished with at least one table and a few stools; and the tables were not just of the trestle type but of the more permanent or 'dormant' kind with legs. Alexander Reynoldson of Writtle, Essex, owned a 'drawing table' or table with leaves in 1671; and some farmers who died at about that date, as did William Garnon of Brant Broughton in Lincolnshire, occasionally possessed a round table. Chairs became commoner as the 17th century advanced; chests, hutches (used for clothes) and boxes were found in most homes. Pewter platters were replacing the wooden trenchers of the Middle Ages. Even George Clinch owned six pieces of pewter. Cooking pots and pans, spits, pothooks, often of elaborate design, and irons and gridirons, pestles and mortars, earthenware pots, and kneading troughs are named in most inventories. Beds, which often stood in the parlour, had low headboards and stout corner posts (like David Bird's bed in the brass in Boxford Church, Suffolk), or they might be four-posters with a canopy. A rich farmer of Roxwell, Henry Turnidge, whose inventory is included in Francis Steer's *Farm and Cottage Inventories of Mid Essex*, boasted a rare carved bedstead. Farmers seem to have slept most often on flock mattresses. Feather beds were a rare luxury, so it is all the pleasanter to know that John Crackett slept on a feather mattress with four pillows and two 'boulsters', a privilege indeed, for in his day pillows and bolsters were still often reserved for women in labour. Crackett's little 'hall' was hung with a painted cloth. Such cloths are commonly mentioned in inventories of the period: Robert Littlefield of Padworth, Berkshire, owned three, as did Thomas Wyhall of Boughton, Kent, in 1569. When hangings could not be afforded walls were still enlivened, as in the Middle Ages, with paintings done directly on the plaster. In an age no longer dominated by ecclesiastical influence, the designs might take the form of repeating patterns, either floral or geometric. The example in a farmhouse at Ashdon, Essex, shows 75 an arrangement of rectangular panels filled with arabesques and strapwork and with undulating briar tendrils climbing up the angles of the room; it was carried out in a range of colours popular at the time – dark green, dull rose and white (now much darkened and faded) – with that occasional deviation from absolute precision which gives such life and immediacy to a hand-painted decoration as opposed to a printed repeating design. The vehicle used for the pigment was glue, probably mixed with egg white.

In many inventories lists of the implements and tools of the farmer and his wife are longer and more detailed than those of household goods. When cloth and linen were spun at home, spinning wheels and sometimes looms, carding stocks and cards for combing out wool or flax were essential possessions. Thus in 1633 Richard Coliard of Thornage, near Holt in Norfolk, owned a spinning 'wheele & a pair of cardes – with a bushel of woole', and Thomas Waynforth of Roydon in the same county also left a spinning wheel and yarn in 1668; while John Addam of Copnall in

75 Painted decoration at Ashdon, Essex, completely covering the walls. The fireplace is of brick.

Staffordshire, who described himself as a yeoman, had two spinning wheels which he kept in the parlour in 1677. The numerous references in inventories to querns, coppers, vats, tubs of all sorts, barrels, hogsheads and malt shovels show that malt was made and beer brewed in many homesteads. Richard Mucklowe of Laphall in Shropshire owned a quern and a number of barrels; William Garnon had a 'brewing vessell' and six barrels; and Bartholomew Burch of Shadoxhurst in Kent, a relatively poor labourer whose home consisted of but hall and hall chamber with an attached dairy and 'drinke hous', owned three tubs and two barrels. The apparatus of the dairy or milkhouse also figures importantly in most inventories. Thomas Waynforth's dairy contained 'an old milke traye or salting traye & a cheese tubb, Eight Cheese fatts [vats], fower breds', a butter cooler and five other coolers, 'Eight old Bowles' and a 'Barrel Chirne'.

Agricultural implements, both hand tools – such as axes, billhooks, mattocks, sickles, spades, rakes, dung forks and pitchforks – and ploughs, harrows, rollers, wagons and carts, which varied according to the type of soil, were naturally prominent items in the list of any farmer's goods. The careful lists of farm animals ('seven Mares and Coltes', 'fower yeere Old Cowes' and 'fower weaneling Calves', '22 lambes yeare owld', 'one breeding mare and two coltes', 'four small horses', 'two old horses and their furniture', 'sixteen dry cows and one bull') show where the owner's chief interest lay. Now and then the names of the animals are recorded, and Swallow, Nut, Py and Marigold graze forever in the fields of Robert Colles, who farmed at South Kilworth in Leicestershire.

The close relationship between traditional farmsteads and cottages and their environment has become abundantly clear in the preceding pages: all the buildings so far described were constructed of materials found in the immediate locality. Something too has been seen of the imaginative development during the Tudor and Stuart periods both of the differences dictated by geology and of the range of possibilities inherent in each type of material. Thus the same basic design might take on the diverging aspects of brick and stone, as it does in the gabled farmhouses at Toseland and $\quad$ 71 Finstock, or emerge in such astonishingly contrasting forms as the brick $\quad$ 70 barn at Hales and the stone barn at Coln Rogers; and half-timber itself $\quad$ 34,28 might show striking variations. It is the craftsman's alert approach to his materials which is chiefly responsible for the vivid impact made by 16th- and 17th-century rural buildings, though other factors played a part in the establishment of local styles.

The trading relations of East Anglia with the Low Countries encouraged the predilection for brick in Norfolk and Suffolk and fostered the fashion in those counties for curved gables like those which, swelling and scrolling above the wings and lofty porch of Red House Farm, Knodishall, deter- $\quad$ 93 mine the whole expansive, stately mood of the house. The Netherlands too were the source of the pantiles which began to undulate on roofs in East Anglia, parts of Lincolnshire and the eastern side of the Vale of York towards the end of the 17th century. Their strong red colour, varied in Norfolk by a shining black which mirrors the blue of summer skies, invigorates many more farm buildings and cottages of the 18th and 19th centuries than of the time when Charles I granted a patent for the making of 'Flanders Tyles'; but those roofing a stable and granary, pigsty and cowshed at Aiskew, Yorkshire, may date from the end of the 17th century, judging from the internal roof structure and the rough character of the wall fabric – dark and light brown gritstone rubble mingled with thin brick, electrified by the sudden blood red of the granary and stable doors.

Maroon or ox red paint for the woodwork – and very often also for the heavy stone frames – of the doors and windows of cottages and farm buildings was traditional in the north, an instinctively felicitous choice in a $\quad$ 147 region of wetness and wildness. Where it persists it draws the eye to the stalwart character of the masonry, emphasizing rude and unconventional detail. The living-room window of a tiny one-storeyed long-house at Skirwith uniquely comprises three separate openings, two minute square-headed windows set immediately against a narrow pointed light. Together they make a lower-case h-shape in reverse, and this bizarre image is forced on the attention of any passer-by and rendered unforgettable by its deep red colour.

Thatch

Where timber and the unbaked earths were the chief available resources they continued to be employed as they had been from the earliest times, generally accompanied by that once ubiquitous and most primitive form of roof covering, thatch. Thatch was still widely found even in stone districts, but it was now used with more sophistication and with regional variations, while the unbaked earths and half-timber became specially associated with the areas to which they were largely relegated. The persistence of thatch for roofing and its common occurrence today, despite antagonistic regulations, are agreeably surprising. No other material so thoroughly sustains the sense of continuity, for thatching is at the same time one of the most ancient of the vernacular crafts and the one which most retains its traditional vigour.

Thatch must be frequently renewed: the life of the most durable variety of thatch, reed, rarely exceeds about eighty years; and whereas the village stonemason, bricklayer and carpenter have either ceased to exist or have been absorbed into commercial firms, the thatcher lives on as an individual craftsman. There are nevertheless fewer thatchers today than at any time and these cover areas far beyond the confines of their own districts, so inevitably some of the sharper regional distinctions must have been blurred or altogether lost. We know, for example, from a study of cottages by G. L. Morris published at the beginning of this century, that marked local differences still existed then between the ornamental disposition of the rods often fastened on top of the thatch at the ridge, eaves and verges as extra protection against wind, that the richest decoration was found in Norfolk and Suffolk, and that in Derbyshire the verges were coated with mortar even though the ridge and eaves might show a pattern of rods. At the present time, the rods generally make a criss-cross design known as 'dimenting' between parallels or are simply arranged in horizontal rows.

The thatcher's methods have been often and well described. Henry Best's account in his *Rural Economy of Yorkshire in 1641* is one of the most detailed and includes an account of the thatching of hayricks, the ridges of which were differently formed from those on houses, for loose straw was used held down by 'twyne hey bands'. C.F. Innocent's investigation of the craft is both thorough and of special interest for his recording of many old local terms still in use in 1916 and now obsolete. The forked instrument used to carry the thatching material up to the roof, generally known as the 'yelm-stick' today, was called the 'bow' in Cambridgeshire, the 'gillet' in Oxfordshire, and the 'groom' in Hertfordshire. Richard Jefferies described the apparatus used by the Wiltshire thatcher and Rider Haggard has preserved the details of the Norfolk thatcher's procedure in *A Farmer's Year*; Tom Hennell gives an artist's graphic description of the thatcher's preparation of his material in *Change on the Farm*, and a whole volume devoted to the craft, *Thatching and Thatched Buildings* by Michael Billett, was published in 1979. Even so, the subject of local and individual styles has never been – and probably can now never be – thoroughly explored.

The materials used in thatching are the straw of the cultivated grasses, wheat, oats and rye; reed, which yields the smoothest finish and most durable covering, and is seen at its best in Norfolk, Suffolk, south-east Cambridgeshire and the Fens; and sometimes, in moorland country where little corn is grown, heather or ling. The board on a master thatcher's cottage at Rockingham, Northamptonshire, announces that he is a specialist in 'Norfolk reed, Devon reed and long straw'. Devon reed, or Dorset reed as it is called in that county, is not reed but a superior kind of

wheat straw, which has not been threshed and has been specially prepared with a device known as a comber. The name by which it is usually known is 'wheat reed'. The term 'long straw' used by Mr Shouler at Rockingham is significant. Straw for thatching, unless it is grown for that purpose, is becoming increasingly difficult to obtain for two reasons: modern strains of wheat are too short in the stalk for thatching, and the combine harvester bruises and crushes the straw. Ideally – and this was the method described by Fitzherbert and followed for three centuries – the straw was grown long and then only the ears were reaped, leaving the tall straw standing to be mown later, or else the ears were cut off after harvest. Characteristic straw thatch can be seen at Bingham's Melcombe in Dorset, Monks Eleigh in Suffolk, and Chipping Campden in Gloucestershire. At Dunsford, Devon, pale, gleaming new thatch of ochre-coloured wheat reed is juxtaposed to sombre heather thatch, stiff as a brush, on roof and wall. Reed proper, smooth as a mole's back, covers the roof of a cottage at Linton, Cambridgeshire, and also that of the thatcher's cottage at Rockingham.

Innocent lists four thatching methods: the material can be sewn to the rafters; pinned to them by means of rods or ledgers (also called 'spars' or 'spicks') which are split wands of willow or hazel, pointed at both ends, or broaches, which are wands of hazel with a twist in the middle so that they resemble huge hairpins; worked into a foundation of turves; or merely held in place by means of a rope mesh, the ends of which are weighted with stones. This last primitive method does not survive in England; from Henry Best's account it seems to have been used only for haystacks even in his day. The second method, very often combined with the first, is the one most commonly followed.

76 *Left* Reed thatch with wheat straw ridge on the master thatcher's cottage, Rockingham, Northamptonshire.

77 *Above* Ornamental reed thatch with wheat straw ridge, Linton, Cambridgeshire. Note the pargework on the dormer gable.

79,78
80

77
76

78 *Left* Wheat straw roof, with a reed and straw dormer, at Monks Eleigh, Suffolk.

79 *Above* Thatched gables at Bingham's Melcombe, Dorset. The hipped gable has a decorative ridge and the suggestion of a little finial.

The straw is tied in bundles known as 'bottles' or 'yelms', which are carefully trimmed and wetted, combed downwards and held in position by rows of ledgers. In the case of wheat reed or reed proper the root ends of the stalks form the exposed surface of the thatch. The yelms are laid slightly diagonally, then combed upwards and attached to the underlying layer of bundles by means of broaches. The first layer of bundles is usually sewn to the rafters with a 12-inch steel needle and tarred rope. Thatchers, like tilers and slaters, work from the eaves upwards and generally from left to right, though the thatcher photographed at Sheepwash, Devon, is working from right to left. This craftsman is using wheat reed on a roof originally thatched with wheat straw. He is wearing traditional leather knee pads which enable him to lean against the rungs of his ladder for hours on end. His tools, apart from the yelm-stick already mentioned, are shears to trim the eaves and a 'patting board' to beat down the thatch. He pushed in the broaches with his hands, but other thatchers sometimes use a mallet. In East Anglia a 'legget' or 'leggatt', a tool consisting of a square, ridged board with a diagonal handle, is used to pat and smooth the thatch.

It seems more than likely that the distinctive ways in which thatch is used, as well as other idiosyncrasies of which traces can yet be seen, emerged during the centuries which are the subject of this chapter. Judging from medieval pictures of thatch it was originally without ornament at the ridge and eaves; in the Middle Ages the ridge was usually covered with clay or turves and the law required that thatched roofs in the vicinity of other buildings should be limewashed to lessen the danger of fire. Furthermore, although dormer windows had appeared before the end of the 15th century

VI

80 *Above* Cob, and thatch of heather and Devon reed, at Dunsford, Devon.

81 *Right* Chalk lump on a clunch base, and straw thatch, at Hadstock, Essex.

they only became common in small dwellings with the widespread introduction of an upper floor, and it was the thatcher's treatment of the dormer as much as his decoration of the ridge which expressed local tradition and his own individuality and skill.

The thatch may be carried straight across the top of the dormer like a gently billowing skirt. This form seems to occur frequently in south Cambridgeshire and north-east Essex, and sometimes on the eastern limestone belt and parts of the Cotswolds, with subtle variations. The dormers of the Rockingham master thatcher's cottage are straight-headed 76 but slope away from the window on either side with conspicuously trim angularity. In Hampshire thatch curves above dormers like thick eyebrows, and in Bedfordshire this curve becomes a sharply defined semicircle, which may be amusingly imitated by tiles when the original thatch has been replaced. A pointed gable habitually crowns the East Anglian dormer and its texture may contrast with that of the roof itself. Reed and straw combine in the dormer thatch of the wheat straw roof at Monks Eleigh. The dormer peeping from the thatch of a chalk lump 78 cottage at Little Sampford, Essex, is unexpectedly roofed with slate, and IV slate fills the spaces between the dormer sills and the eaves line.

The thatcher's treatment of gables varies as much as his approach to the dormer. He may regard the hipped gable as an exaggerated version of the dormer, as he does on one of the wings of a farmhouse at Bingham's Melcombe; or he may simply frame the gable with a neatly cut inverted V of thatch, as on the other wing at Bingham's Melcombe; or instead of treating the hipped gable as a single rounded shape, he may visualize the hip as a

Opposite
IX Moat Farm, Great
Tey, Essex: a
Georgianized farmhouse,
standing on an ancient
site. (See p. 149.)

separate entity, as at Elsenham, and draw up the thatch at either end of the ridge in a pert, pyramidal finial.

The most accomplished thatchers delight in a type of ridge ornament which is more ostentatious and more complicated than the limited rod decoration. The protective cap of thatch along the ridge, usually of wheat straw or perhaps of sedge, for Norfolk reed is too tough to be bent over the ridge, makes a pattern which is always a play upon the scallop, the V-shaped tongue and the half hexagon, and which is obviously related to the carved and moulded ornament of the Tudor and Stuart periods. The pattern may be repeated some way down the slope of the roof, as it is on the cottage at Linton. Here the beautiful precision of the ornamental reed thatch finely contrasts with a display of wattle design pargetting on a shining white dormer.

Formerly the thatcher would celebrate the completion of his work by setting a corn dolly on the ridge or gable. A thatcher at work at Buckland-in-the-Moor in the 1950s was making a Devonshire cross to put on the gable, and at that time a cock perched proudly on the ridge of a cottage at Ebrington, a village where the remarkable display of thatch above Cotswold stone walls perfectly demonstrates the suitability of this ancient and homely roofing material for every variety of rural dwelling.

Buildings made of earth

Buildings of earth are now found mostly in the West Country, in East Anglia and occasionally in the mild chalkland valleys and hills of Wiltshire, Berkshire, the South Downs, Hampshire and Buckinghamshire. The earth is known by varying local names: 'cob' in the south-west, especially in Dorset and Devon, 'witchit' or 'wichert' in Buckinghamshire, 'chalk lump' and 'clay lump' in East Anglia. Perhaps these names may have been coined in the period when the rural builder first became vividly conscious of regional diversities in the stuffs with which he was working, for the earliest use Innocent found of the word 'cob' or 'clob' was in a 17th-century Devonshire inventory.

The methods of preparing the earth were roughly the same in all districts and have been well described by witnesses. S. O. Addy gave an account in 1898 of the construction of a mud cottage at Mappleton in the East Riding of Yorkshire, and the architect Claude Messent watched the proceedings for the erection of a clay lump farm building in south Norfolk in 1926. The earth was dug near the site of the building, spread out in a layer about a foot thick, thoroughly watered, then mixed with straw and trodden by a horse or ox – though I was told by an elderly labourer who had himself worked on the restoration of a chalk lump cottage at Ashdon that the treading was traditionally done by the workmen in north-west Essex. The process was known as 'tempering'. Where chalk was at hand it was crunched up with the mixture; in Cornwall small pieces of broken slate, called 'shilf', were added, one load of shilf to two of clay; and in the heathy districts of Dorset and Devon sand and gravel strengthened the clay.

There were two ways of building the walls. In both cases the first step was to construct a plinth about $1\frac{1}{2}$ or 2 feet high (though it was often much less). This might be made of rubble, as at Dunsford in Devon and Mullion

in Cornwall, or of pebbles, flint or brick, as at Duddenhoe End in Essex and Bryant's Puddle in Dorset. A cottage at Hadstock, Essex, built of chalk lump, is set on a plinth of clunch or chalk stone, the dazzlingly white, tractable limestone of Cambridgeshire and north-west Essex. The mixture might then be laid upon the plinth in courses with a dung fork, the thickness of the material, according to Addy, being about 5 to 7 inches. The walls at Selworthy, Somerset, where the whole village is of cob, are at least 2 feet thick and the walls of a cottage at Tacolneston, Norfolk, are about 18 inches thick. The courses diminished in height as the wall rose, the first course being about 2½ feet high. Each course was forked up when wet and pliant, thinly covered with straw, trampled down by the workmen and left to dry before the next course was added. The lintels of doors and window frames, if they were of wood rather than stone, were set in position as the work went along and sometimes cupboards would be fitted at the same time. Alternatively, the prepared mixture was put into wooden moulds and shaped into large blocks about 18 inches long, 6 inches deep and 9 inches wide for external walls, and smaller blocks about 12 inches long, 6 inches deep and 6 inches wide for internal walls. The blocks were turned out after a few days, then left for several months to dry thoroughly.

Whichever of the two methods was chosen the process was slow: it might take as long as two years to complete a two-storeyed building, so it is not surprising that the greater number of surviving earthen structures are very small farm buildings or cottages of one storey with an attic floor above. Nevertheless some rural craftsmen of the great age of vernacular building attempted designs of a more ambitious scale and character. Parsonage Farm, Burwell, the arresting shape of which has been remarked, 67 is built of chalk lump with windows and door frames of clunch. The manor of Hayes Barton, the home of Sir Walter Raleigh at East Budleigh in Devon, translates into earth and thatch a form of hall-house design – the E-plan with a central porch and far advancing wings embracing a courtyard – usually reserved for great houses such as Barrington Court, Somerset; and a large farmhouse at Mundham, Norfolk, displays an exciting, sparsely fenestrated gabled façade with a tall staircase projection pressed against a low, long cross-wing and two colossal brick chimneystacks. The fireplaces inside this house are also of brick, some with moulded ornament, but in chalk country the chimneystacks and the fireplaces may be fashioned of clunch, as in the cottage at Duddenhoe End just cited and in a farmhouse at Elmdon, both in Essex.

The walls of earthen buildings naturally varied in colour according to regional distinctions in the character of the clay. Harrison observed that clay was either 'white, red or blue; and of these the first doth participate very much with the nature of our chalk, the second is called loam, but the third eftsoons changeth colour so soon as it is wrought, notwithstanding that it look blue when it is thrown out of the pit'. But usually the colour of the earth is concealed under a coating of plaster or roughcast and limewash. Roughcast, which consisted of coarse sand, slaked lime and shingle, gravel XIV or other material, even cinders, was, as the name suggests, thrown on to the walls with a flat trowel. It may be seen on cottages at Bryant's Puddle, for instance, and at Melbourn in Cambridgeshire.

Opposite
X At St Clement, near Truro, Cornwall, a cottage guards the entrance to the churchyard, which is effected through a passage in the granite and slatestone ground floor. Above the passage is a slate-hung structure with 'Gothick' windows, used as a parish room or schoolhouse.

82 Close studding at Church Farm, Stebbing, Essex.

83 Square panels and bold patterns at Old Hall Farm, Woodford, Cheshire.

Timber-framing

A tentative outline of the construction of timber-framed walls was given in the earlier account of medieval farmsteads. The methods employed in developed timber building have been the focus of much recent expert investigation, so only the more salient features of regional styles will be discussed here. The timber frames manifesting these styles, which in the Middle Ages were no more than faintly adumbrated but which now burst forth with fantastical divergencies in the different areas with which this form of building was specifically associated, have been compared unfavourably by some authorities with the structurally more substantial products of the Middle Ages, yet these late examples of the carpenter's art, exploring as they do all the inherent decorative potentialities of the medium, make a most dramatic contribution to the visual delights of the countryside. We have seen the contrast between the narrowly spaced, ashen-hued stripes of East Anglian timber-work and the cruck framing, black-and-white square panelling and exuberant patterning of the West Midlands. A glance at Church Farm, Stebbing, the gable end of a cottage at Weobley, and Old Hall Farm at Woodford, with its lattices of cusped timbers, ornamental coving, cusped lozenges, stripes and bold zigzags, confirms the distinction. Close studding and square panels can both be seen in Kent and east Sussex, and romantic Castwizzel Manor, near Biddenden, is a particularly fine example of the former. Decorative panelling and close studding are combined at Sedlescombe Manor, Sussex, formerly a farm and

82

5,83

now three cottages, but such ornament never in this area achieves the force and vivacity of a façade like that of Oak Farm at Styal.   65

The material of the wattle-and-daub filling of the panels varied according to the type of clay available, and intriguing regional names emphasized the differences. In Kent daubing was referred to as 'loaming'; in Cheshire wattle and daub went by the name of 'raddle and daub' or 'rad and dab'; in the West Country wattle work was known as 'freeth' or 'vreath', while in East Anglia the rods were called 'rizzes' or 'razors' and Essex churchwardens' accounts employ the terms 'splint' and 'stovett'. Innocent suggests that 'vreath' may be a variant of 'wreath'; and in a dictionary of 1602 'rathel' or 'raddle' is given as cognate with 'harthel' or 'hurdle'. In early timber-framed buildings, such as Pattenden, the filling was set back from the timber frame, but in a house of the date of Church   82
Farm, Stebbing, the panels are usually flush with the frame.

Laths replaced wattle in later timber structures, and when older framed farmhouses were enlarged and restored in the 16th and 17th centuries the panels might be filled with materials other than wattle and daub. Oak Farm   65
at Styal and Rose Cottage at Coalbrookdale, Shropshire (altered in 1642), both include panels filled with brick and stone rubble, all limewashed to preserve the black-and-white pattern favoured in the region. So tenaciously did West Midland craftsmen cling to this tradition that sometimes if a house were built entirely of brick they would adorn it with a painted semblance of timber panels. A brick addition to Old Hall Farm, Woodford, shows this extraordinary decoration. Brick replaced wattle and daub in the frame of the great Wheat Barn at Cressing Temple when it was rebuilt for the last time, and restorers used brick for many of the panels at Lower Brockhampton. Chalk lump can be seen between the timbers of the   I
hayloft at Parsonage Farm, Burwell.

Brick, because it was a novelty and fashionable at the time, was the alternative most preferred to wattle and daub. The most popular arrangement of the bricks between the timbers was the herringbone pattern: the narrow bricks of the 16th century zigzagging up and down the panels, improbably clasped by the contrasting timbers, can impart a most exotic air to a façade, especially if, as in the case of a cottage at Water Stratford, Buckinghamshire, the building is thatched and the bricks display   VII
irregularities in texture and colour. Here they range from dark plum red to palest terracotta. Sometimes the bricks are laid in the normal way, while at others diagonal courses between closely set timbers may be combined with horizontal courses in square and rectangular panels, as at Charendon Farm in Warwickshire.

The East Anglian custom of wholly encasing a timber-framed house in a   53–56
sheath of plaster no doubt developed as a means of defeating the draughts   67,68
which found their way through the timber frame as both the wood and the wattle shrank with age. Many medieval farmhouses and cottages were plastered in the 16th and 17th centuries. Timber-framed dwellings built in   23
the 17th century were generally encased in plaster from the outset because by then the timber used might well be inferior. There was a further, aesthetic, reason for the custom: smooth walls accorded better with growing classical tastes than the narrowly spaced stripes and insistent   82

84, 85 Late timber-framed cottages at Boughton, Kent, before and after 'restoration' – the removal of the coat of plaster and insertion of 'antique' windows and door.

verticality of East Anglian timber frames. Gleaming white or painted the traditional pink, buff, ochre or deep red, these plastered farmhouses and cottages remain as characteristic of the gentle East Anglian landscape as they were when Constable saw them as inseparable from his vision of Suffolk. The present fashion of stripping off the plaster sheath to expose the timbers can seldom be justified, even when it reveals medieval timbers that were originally exposed; but when the seemly covering is torn from rough work and poor timbers, and when an air of antiquity is falsely suggested by alterations to doors and windows, as for instance at Boughton in Kent, the result is aesthetically, practically and historically outrageous.

84,85

The astonishing distinction between timber-framed houses such as Oak Farm at Styal and Westbury Farm at Ashwell is heightened when the plaster is embellished with the ornament it so clearly invites. Although a gild of 'plaisterers' had been formed in London as early as 1501, the craft only reached its full development in the 17th century, with the emergence of external plaster ornament. Known as 'pargetting' or 'pargework', this decoration is a peculiarly English phenomenon associated particularly with Suffolk and Essex and the adjacent counties of Cambridgeshire and Hertfordshire. Sporadic instances do occur here and there in Norfolk and also in Herefordshire, where one of the gables of the Ley at Weobley displays a plaster sun head and a spray of thistles and oak leaves. The work may, like the well-known frieze on Bishop Bonner's Cottages at East Dereham, Norfolk, be raised in colour on a neutral ground, but the design is generally and most effectively conceived as white on white or buff on buff like the embroidery on the white or cream counterpanes that once graced cottage homes. The word 'pargetting' originally indicated any form of plaster sheath and in his *London Prices* of 1750 Batty Langley still uses it in this broad sense; it seems to have been restricted to external ornamental plasterwork only in the early years of the present century.

64

Traditional external plaster was composed of lime, sand, cow hair and cow dung, sometimes with the addition of chopped straw and stable manure. The resulting mixture was extremely tough and, unlike modern plaster which is mixed with cement and dries in a few minutes, fairly slow drying so that the pargetter had ample time to garnish the surface. The simplest adornment took the form of panels, perhaps suggested by the oak panelling which was the usual form of wall covering in the most important rooms of timber-framed houses from the first quarter of the 16th century. Usually the borders of these panels are recessed, an effect achieved by placing thin wooden templates on the surface of the last but one coat of plaster, then bringing up the plaster to the level of the templates before removing them. Occasionally roughcast might be used for this last coat, thus creating a contrast in texture such as can be seen on a cottage in Shilling Street, Lavenham. Small flints set in projecting panels give sudden unexpected prominence to a modest little dwelling in Saffron Walden. Less frequently, the panels themselves are recessed, leaving the borders in relief, a device which can be seen on a cottage at Ashwell.

Some of the panels at Ashwell exhibit huge scroll ornaments in deep relief and this is the most exotic form of pargework. Designs such as the ravishing honeysuckly frieze and panels of Tudor roses enriching a cottage at Sibton, Suffolk, and the flatter but much more intricate pattern of 161 arabesques, cartouches, rosettes and bell flowers that coils over great segments of the upper walls of a former farmhouse at Earls Colne, Essex, were executed by means of wooden or wax moulds. The giant sprays of leaves and flowers which cannot fail to catch the eye of anyone walking or driving along Nethergate Street in Clare, Suffolk, clambering all over a 86 cottage wall and gable, were modelled by hand with the aid of a trowel, a much smaller tool than the one used to apply the plaster sheath to the walls, the flowing lines having first been described in rope on the last but one coat of plaster. The craftsman would be holding the plaster in his left hand on a square trencher-like tool known as a 'hawke'.

Another less insistent but equally lively form of decoration, free and calligraphic, can be seen on the walls of a yeoman farmhouse, Hubbard's Hall at Bentley in Suffolk. For this the plasterer has used a pointed stick as if it were a burin to incise spontaneous representations of daisies in scallop-edged panels and small motifs of wavy lines, crosses and curving lozenge shapes. Sometimes a pretty pattern would be made by just pricking the plaster with a stick, and there is a delightful example of this on a cottage wall at Coggeshall in Essex; often a fan of pointed sticks, or a comb, would be used to create the most frequently occurring motifs – shell-shapes, zigzags and undulations. Frequently in north-west Essex a square wooden mould cut with three bars was pressed this way and that into the moist plaster to produce a pattern resembling wattling. Cottages everywhere in this district show this rudimentary design, while others display an all-over four-petalled flower pattern made by pressing a similar square mould into the plaster. At least one local craftsman still cuts moulds of this simple kind and uses them in the traditional way when the decorative plaster on an old cottage must be renewed. The hard, mechanical effect of such renewals is due to the nature of the quick-drying modern plaster.

86 Pargework at Clare, Suffolk.

Very occasionally at the end of the 17th century the plaster sheath of a house might be incised or moulded to simulate the appearance of masonry blocks: the walls of cottages at Steeple Bumpstead were treated in this way, although the pattern is almost obliterated by successive coats of limewash and the present leprous state of the plaster. But such imitation properly belongs to a later period when ever greater emphasis was put upon the stone façade.

Yet other methods were devised for protecting timber-framed walls, increasing at the same time the rich variety of their aspect. In Kent, east Sussex, Surrey, Essex, Suffolk and parts of Hertfordshire and Cambridgeshire clapboard made its appearance towards the end of the 17th century, the boards being pegged or, later, nailed to the studding. The tradition was ancient, for Innocent found oak weatherboarding of great age on a cruck house at Ewden, Yorkshire, and traces of former clapboarding in the fabric of medieval northern cottages, the walls of which had been rebuilt later in stone. This seems interestingly to show that like half-timber itself weatherboarding was only relegated to particular regions during the periods of rebuilding. In the earliest East Anglian and south-eastern examples, such as the barn and granary at Arrington, Cambridgeshire, the boards are irregular and follow the line of the tree's growth. They may be haphazardly spaced, as they are on the least restored section of the walls of the great barn at Wendens Ambo, Essex, and on those of a tumbledown cottage at Tenterden, Kent, where they jostle for place with brick-nogged panels. In all these instances the boards are tarred. The sable walls of Essex and Suffolk barns, roofed with steep thatch or mossed tiles, and the frequent groups of black farm buildings clustered alongside a white plastered farmhouse, as at Abbess Roding, stand out 32 against ripe cornfields or the green of spring with dramatic, almost abstract severity.

If it was not tarred the weatherboarding on farmhouses and cottages was traditionally painted white, as it is on two cottages at Nuthampstead, Hertfordshire, in one of which it is combined with a plaster sheath, a common occurrence. The boards here are made of elm, the wood generally used for this form of walling, and are laid with fair precision, regularly overlapping to cast thin lines of shadow and encourage a marked horizontal effect. This characteristic was to be deliberately developed as the horizontal mode became more dominant; and weatherboarding, as the following chapter of this book will disclose, is seen at its most sophisticated 114 in buildings of the Georgian and Regency periods.

In the Weald of Kent, in Surrey and Sussex and now and then in the neighbouring counties of Berkshire and Hampshire, timber-framed farmhouses and cottages were weatherproofed by tile-hanging, the warm, russet-hued material deepening the congeniality and intimacy of a mellow countryside of orchards, tufted hills and hopfields. These wall tiles, not made prior to the 17th century, were flatter and thinner than those used on roofs. They were fastened to the laths with pins of hazel, willow or elder and bedded in lime and hair mortar. While the gable end, if it faced east or north, was often completely tile-hung, only the upper floor of the façades was generally protected, especially if it were jettied. The ground floor might be plastered, half-timbered, or encased in brick. The most harmonious effects are those created when roof and walls, crowned by a brick chimneystack of the same hue, are covered with tiles of a uniform, glowing texture. But just as the plasterer was excited by the marvellous decorative potentiality of his material so the tile-maker responded to the seductive possibilities of pattern. Walls were overlaid with fish scales, with alternating rows of beak shapes and semicircles, or, as at Capel, Surrey, 87 with strangely flanged tiles creating a vigorously chiaroscuroed fret, which here consorts uncomfortably with a massive roof of sandstone slates quarried below the North Downs nearby. When sandstone presses upon clapboard the contrast is still more marked.

In the West Country the few timber-framed houses which were not rebuilt in stone were, from the 17th century onwards, hung with slates. No one looking at a Cornish roof and slate-enveloped wall would immediately X,117 connect this hard, tightly textured, brown-grey, sky-reflecting stone with mud and shale, but that is the composition of slate: mud and shale metamorphosed by enormous heat and unimaginable pressures more than three hundred million years ago. Craftsmen from the time of the Roman occupation onwards recognized the obvious usefulness of a rock so easily split, and the late E.M. Jope discovered that slates quarried in Cornwall and Devon were being transported to south and south-eastern England for roofing ecclesiastical buildings as early as 1187. The famous Delabole quarry near Camelford was opened during Elizabeth I's reign, and the

87 Decorative tile-hanging and a sandstone roof, Capel, Surrey.

material may have come from there for the many slate-hung cottages and farmhouses in and near St Columb Major. The slates on a house in that village are attractively patterned, two rows of plain slates alternating with two of half octagonal shape and a contrasting blue-grey colour and with triangular and diamond-shaped panels interrupting the regular lines of slates. That device is seen also on the upper tier of a three-storeyed row of slate-hung timber-framed cottages at Dunster, Somerset. The overlapping slates were generally attached to battens. The slater's tools, according to R. Holme's *Academy of Armory and Blazon* published in 1688, were 'Hatchet, Trowel, Hewing Knife, Pick to Hole, Pinning Iron to widen the Holes, Hewing Block, Lathing Measure, and Stone *Do.*, and Pins, Stone nails or Lath Nails and Laths or Latts'.

Thicker slates of a different colour, green-grey rather than brown-grey or blue-grey, were quarried in Cumberland and are found not only on the walls of Lake District farm buildings and farmhouses but also, though rarely, on the walls. The upper part of the porch of Fellfoot Farm, for instance, is timber-framed and slate-hung, the rows of plain slates varied by a wooden panel bearing a carved criss-cross pattern, painted black.

62

Stone

The diversities in texture and style of the stone buildings which were replacing earlier, flimsier structures on the farm and in the village during the housing revolution of the 16th and 17th centuries have already found their way into these pages. The contrasts between the oolitic limestone and urbane aspect of the farm buildings at Ablington or Bibury in 48,31 Gloucestershire, the carboniferous limestone and primitive strength of the cowbyre and hayloft at Alport in Derbyshire, and the sombre texture and 41 weight of the northern sandstone of the cowbyres and stables at Blencarn in 40 Cumberland, each in accord with its setting, strike the eye all the more forcibly because of basic similarities in structure. A comparison between a farmhouse such as that at Great Barrington and cottages at Kettlewell in 89,90 Yorkshire, where the rubble has been roughcast but where the dripstones coarsely recall the Cotswold style, reveals them, both made of limestone but differently constituted and of different origin, to be as distinct as the encompassing landscapes, green and gently undulating on the one hand, high treeless moor on the other. The reddish purple colour of the sandstone at Blencarn is not common in the north, where this rock, usually known as millstone grit, is of a forbidding grey, sometimes speckled, and found in 30 blocks of cyclopean proportions which are maintained when the stone is dressed – as it is at Highlow Hall Farm, Abney, Derbyshire. Here the hugely crenellated farmhouse is approached and dramatically opposed by a heavy arched gateway, a local mason's personal interpretation of a classical theme, incorporating short, eccentric columns in the upper stage, giant balls, and a curving pediment sprouting scrolls and topped by a sphere. The red Devonian sandstone of the south-west, of which the ground-floor walls of the slate-hung cottages at Dunster are made, is of quite another character, warm brown and rufous of hue and close in texture.

The greater number of traditional stone farmsteads are composed of varieties of limestone and sandstone; but in parts of the north and the south-west granite and ancient volcanic rock have been laboriously fashioned into domestic shells. Awareness of the stubborn resistance of the granite to the mason's will is the first sensation experienced in front of a building such as the farmhouse of Penfound near the north coast of Cornwall; the porch, in which a brave attempt has been made to shape and mould the stone, stands out against the rough walls, adorned with a painfully cut coat of arms in the faintest relief and the scarcely discernible date 1642. The house seems as close to nature as the ruins of Chysauster. 3 This closeness is always felt with particular intensity when those rocks are used which have come from titanic upheavings of the heavier, lower materials of the earth. The whole village of Morvah, as it looked a quarter of a century ago, might have risen by a natural process from its igneous foundations, and in the same way the stable at Brimmerhead, of granite, 46 slatestone rubble and lava, seems to grow from the rock. All the wildness of the Cumbrian fells lies concentrated in the walls of Cheery Nook at 59 Matterdale. Rough lumps of dark grey lava, brown tufa and dour slate-stone rubble laid without mortar form the gable end, their barbaric aspect only a little tamed on the façade by a modicum of mortar and a coat of limewash.

88 Sarsen is the material both of the prehistoric monoliths and of a cottage at Avebury, Wiltshire.

With younger, more easily worked stones, the sense of order and of the human element is stronger than the overwhelming consciousness of nature. But the affinity with place remains, often making a memorable impression when the stone comes from one of the more uncommon formations. Buildings of that odd, toffee-coloured and toffee-textured XIII sandstone called carstone can never be seen without a sense of surprise as great as that inspired by the strange variegated cliffs of Old Hunstanton in Norfolk where the material is splendidly displayed in its natural state. It was not much used for entire walls before the 18th century, though it does make an earlier appearance as small random lumps on walls of mixed substances like the gable end of Bishop Bonner's Cottages, East Dereham. 88 Again the kinship of a cottage at Avebury, Wiltshire, with its setting is notably proclaimed by its fabric, for it is the same grey sandstone as that of the Bronze Age monoliths in the shadow of which it stands. Found as great boulders on the downs, the stones are called sarsens, from Saracen, because of their alien character.

The renowned limestone 'belt' ranges irregularly from the Purbeck Downs in Dorset, across Somerset, the Cotswolds and the Northampton-shire uplands into south Lincolnshire and up into east Yorkshire, where at Middleton-by-Pickering lively, shelly, rough-textured cottage walls support roofs of pantiles. Here the limestone is of a cool grey colour; in the Cotswolds it is of a honied and creamy rather than silvery pallor, though at XII Great Tew and Barford St Michael it becomes a rich ochre yellow. In Northamptonshire and Rutland the rock may again be impregnated with VIII iron, and the pale and the stained, nutty brown stone are sometimes set in alternate courses to produce horizontally striped walls. The limestone of Somerset and Dorset is of a delicate grey-gold. The stone farm buildings of this area, so many of them still untouched, are profoundly evocative of older farming traditions.

89 Carboniferous limestone at Kettlewell, Yorkshire, takes form in heavy roofing slates and coarse mouldings. Note the pigeon holes under the eaves.

90 Characteristic use of oolitic limestone in the Cotswolds: rubble walls, stone slates, dormer-gables, mullioned windows, drip mouldings and ashlared chimneys at Great Barrington, Gloucestershire.

It is in the Cotswolds above all that oolitic limestone (so-called because the most typical deposits look like masses of fish-roe) dominates the scene and it was here that skilled masons with a copious supply of fine, easily worked stone from countless small local quarries established and perfected a vernacular style in which traditional and classical motifs were fused in a unique synthesis. The style was retained throughout the 18th and part of the 19th centuries for farmhouse and cottage buildings, so that despite all the self-consciousness of such show villages as Broadway and Bourton-on-the-Water, the Cotswolds present the face of 17th-century rural England more clearly than any other part of the country. The components of the style – the mullioned windows surmounted by square dripstones of Tudor style, the ball-topped finials, the oval or circular decorative panels, the prominence of gable and gablet, the elegant proportions of the square chimneystacks – have already been noticed. Stone porches, arched and protected by a hood mould, might distinguish the most unpretentious cottages; and the ground floor was usually flagged.

The infinite divergencies in the textures of stone walls are not only due to differences in the grain, colour and composition of the many varieties of stone: the stone itself can be treated in a number of ways, each of which brings out special qualities of the material. Most cottages and farm buildings are built of rubble – stone which has been left as found or only slightly dressed. Some stones, like that of which the Matterdale farmstead is built, are too intractable to be shaped and they are used without order other than that the largest stones are placed near the base of the wall. Such irregular stones may be laid without mortar; in the long-houses of the north the distinction between the quarters of animals and men is often marked by the treatment of the masonry, dry-stone walling for the cowbyre and stone bedded in mortar for the house, as at Little Langdale. A most interesting and vigorous texture was obtained when the mortar was used sparsely and set back, though the lively effects of this technique have nearly always been impaired by later infillings of mortar and even cement. Both textures, random rubble masonry as it was originally laid and as it looks with all its sparkle dimmed after cementing, appear in the walls of the Hawkswick field house seen earlier.

Sometimes the rubble may be roughly squared, as it partly is in the wall of a cottage at Great Tew, and sometimes it may be squared and dressed but not faced with smooth thinly cut stone as it is in the grandest buildings – though when the stone permits, this finish is used for the frames of doors and windows, wherever they are not constructed of wood, and for quoins. The ashlared walls of the pigsty at Chipping Campden attest to its aristocratic origin, and a cottage near Meon Hill may owe the fine smooth surface of its walls to loftier beginnings. Toller Farm, Toller Fratrum, Dorset, shows a patchwork of ashlared masonry, squared and partly dressed stone and squared rubblestone. It is the living quality of walling stones which have been dressed but not ashlared which makes a cottage in Broadway remain in the memory. The touch of the mason is warmly, strongly present in the façade of this little building – it quite literally embodies his procedures, the selection of blocks in the quarry, the careful examination of each one and the choice of a surface from which to square

91 Cottage at Broadway, Worcestershire.

the rest; the dressing of the rough stones with the chisels and punch whose marks they bear; and then the picking over of the differently sized stones to decide the exact place of each one in the close-fitting jigsaw of the wall.

The serene visual character of Cotswold farms and villages depends very much on the complete harmony of walls and roofs. The eye is never startled in this gracious region by the sudden contrast of half-timber and ponderous sandstone slates (as at Oak Farm, Styal), by the sight of even heavier stone slates above decorative tiles (as at Capel, Surrey), or by the unexpected change from big Purbeck stone slates and conspicuous mortar to tiles on a single roof (as at Toller Fratrum, Dorset). The limestone slates of the steeply pitched Cotswold roofs are of exquisite, not in the least mechanical regularity; and though they are in fact of tremendous weight, they could not look more unlike the thick, obviously massy slates of the low-pitched roofs of the Lake District and the north. The slates vary in size, diminishing as they approach the eaves. Like the thatcher, the mason worked from left to right and began at the eaves. It was probably when they were first widely used, in the 16th and 17th centuries, that the slates were given the apt and fanciful names which changed with the region. Randle Holme tells us the names of slates 'according to their Several Lengths' used in the north in 1688: 'Short Haghattee, Long Haghattee, Farwells, Chilts, Warnetts, Shorts, Shorts save one or Shorts so won, Short Backs, Long Backs, Batchlers, Wivetts, Short Twelves, Long Twelves, Jenny why Gettest thou, Rogue why Winkest thou'. In the Cotswolds the slates bore such names as 'cocks', 'cuttings', 'nobbities', 'becks', 'bachelors', 'nines' and 'hibbuts', 'elevens', 'sixteens', 'follows' and 'eaves'. In this area the ridges might be sawn out of the stone; but where the stone was less tractable, in the Lake District, the ridge slates were laid alternately on each side of the roof, notched and then locked together. Such slates were, from the time of Elizabeth I, appropriately known as 'wrestlers'.

65
87

70,90

Stone roof slates were originally bedded on hay, straw or bog moss and fastened to the rafters with oak pegs. Before mortar replaced the vegetable material it was the custom for a 'mosser' or 'moser', known also as the 'moss man', to make periodic inspections of stone-slated roofs: if the moss had decayed he would use a heavy square-ended trowel called the 'mossing iron' to poke new moss between as well as under the slates to keep out draughts and snow. In the Lake District the house leek, there called the aye-green, was also common on roofs and was grown above doors and windows as well. Thriving without soil and thought to have come from the Near East and to have magical healing powers, this plant was cherished as a generator of vitality and as a safeguard against thunder and lightning, just as the iron horseshoe, nailed above so many farmhouse, stable and cottage doors, was regarded as a sure protection against evil, a survival of the ancient veneration of the strange metal which in the far past had vanquished the race of stone- and bronze-weaponed peoples.

Brick

The tall, bedizened chimney-columns still announcing the presence of so many of the farmhouses and cottages which are the subject of this chapter are some of the more astounding of the inventions prompted by the revived use of brick. And brick, although much later, when commercially exploited, inimical to vernacular styles and materials, was at first as lively and as immediate a manifestation of place as stone or chalk lump. Bricks were made locally in simple kilns. As we have seen, they varied in colour with the nature of the available clay, from every shade of red to the pale yellow found in excessively limy districts like south Cambridgeshire. The undulating floor of Tiptofts, Wimbish, in another limy area, north-west

92 The hall floor of Tiptofts, Wimbish, Essex (see ill. 18).

93 Imposing curving Dutch gables of 17th-century brickwork at Red House Farm, Knodishall, Suffolk.

Essex (one of the brick floors which, where stone flags were unobtainable, were beginning to replace ground floors of mud), is palest ochre suffused with delicate pink. This floor shows all the enchanting eccentricity, the slight imperfections in the bricks – creases and indentations due to inadequately controlled methods of firing – and the arbitrary system of laying them, rows of stretchers suddenly changing direction and as suddenly interrupted by rows of bricks set face upwards instead of on edge, which imparts such animation to early brickwork. The lack of uniformity in wall after wall of this period is a source of considerable visual pleasure.

No special method of laying or bonding the bricks was consistently adopted until at least the end of the 17th century. In Suffolk, at Flemings Hall, Bedingfield, headers alternate with rows of stretchers, in an arrangement known as English bond; at Red House Farm, Knodishall, a row of stretchers is succeeded by a row of headers, then by three rows of stretchers, and then a row of two stretchers alternating with one header is followed by one of two headers alternating with one stretcher; the walls of the barn at Hales are enlivened by bands of projecting headers, and here alternating rows of stretchers and headers consort with rows laid quite haphazardly.

93

34

A uniquely decorated brick façade compels attention at Wheatley, Nottinghamshire. The builder of a farmhouse there dated 1673 was carried away by the classical details he may have seen in some of the French and Netherlandish handbooks which had been circulating throughout the century, or may have observed on some of the great houses in his neighbourhood. The improbable, illogical façade wonderfully communicates his pleasure in rendering these motifs in brick and arranging them to suit his sprightly fancy. Extraordinarily tall pilasters – shapes in relief banded by projecting stretchers, their capitals an attempt at the Ionic order in rubbed and carved brick – flank the low arch of the porch and support nothing. Above them hovers a broad entablature of moulded and projecting bricks and from that, each set on a pair of brick roundels, two absurd obelisks rise in relief on either side of a lunette. The entablature is carried right across the façade and the lunette is repeated by a row of like shapes – semicircular pediments – partly made in wooden moulds, looping heavily along and finishing disconcertingly but deliberately with a half lunette at either end.

Flint

One of the most visually exciting building materials, flint, began to enrich the exteriors of cottages and farm buildings at about the same time as brick. Flint, like thatch, belongs to a tradition rooted in prehistory, for the flint knapping industry of Brandon in Suffolk, which only came to an end a year or two ago, was established by our Neolithic forebears. A mysterious and exceptionally hard silica, found in nodules of suggestive shapes, as though produced by stupendous pressure on molten matter, or in bands in the chalk districts of East Anglia, Sussex, Dorset and Wiltshire, flint gives local character to the medieval parish churches of Norfolk and Suffolk, but was not used for small domestic buildings in the Middle Ages because the corners and the angles of doors and window frames could not be managed without the support of another material, and the stone which was combined with flint for ecclesiastical work was not available for cottages and barns. But with the re-introduction of brick and the much wider use of stone for secular buildings farmsteads began to take shape in flint. The material was either gathered from the fields and used in its rough state or quarried and knapped, the process by which the craftsman shaped the flints for building, using different hammers, and squared them to different sizes, revealing the jet black or mixed coloured hearts of the stones.

Flint may occasionally be associated with bones in walls as late as the 19th century. Some flints indeed look like bone, and a horse bone takes its place almost unnoticed in a cottage wall at Cley-next-the-Sea, Norfolk. It perpetuates an ancient custom according to which bones were incorporated in the fabric of a house to ward off evil, for the virtue of a good horse was thought by this means to enter into the building and protect it.

By far the greater number of flint farmhouses and cottages found in the villages of Norfolk and Suffolk and parts of the southern counties were built in the 18th and 19th centuries, but some examples are of earlier date and are already informed with something of the originality and spirit which are particularly associated with this challenging and unusual material. The

village of Castle Acre, which lies in the district where the flint knapping industry was centred, contains several flint cottages dating from Tudor and Stuart times. The stones of some of these have been used in their rough state, while those of others have been quartered (the first stage in the knapping process). The walls are reinforced with brick and also with fragments of masonry from the ruins of the great Priory at the end of the village street. Blocks of ashlared stone play a still larger part in the walls of a cottage near Hyde Abbey, Hampshire, where they form a rough chequer pattern with flints intermingled with brick here and there. A 17th-century farmhouse at Trunch exhibits walls such as everywhere delight the eye in north-west Norfolk, made of small, close-set, rounded flint pebbles called cobbles and forming a texture like plain knitting. The stones, coated with a white patina of chalk, set off the brilliant red of the prominent brick chimney clusters and the patterned arrangement of the quoins and gable edges. The glinting, cobbled gable end of a row of one-storeyed cottages at Lakenheath in Suffolk is spotted with brick headers and set with diamond shapes in brick, one within the other. The walls of a cottage at Bingham's Melcombe, where the small, roughly squared flints, laid in even courses, are of a chalky brown colour, are banded by double rows of brick at intervals. Much larger and wilder field flints join with brick to make a barn at East Raynham, Norfolk, and to form the background for a charming piece of decoration: ventilation is provided by a window filled with alternating spaces and stretchers, the bold red bricks held together by white, pebble-like dollops of mortar where they overlap.

It has not been possible here to point to more than a few of such individual contrivances. They defy classification, but it is their like, so richly abundant in every region, which, while the bulldozer is held at bay, makes the exploration of local craftsmen's ways with their materials a source of such perennial surprise and untrammelled delight.

94 *Above left* Flint, brick and fragments of stone from the Priory ruins at Castle Acre, Norfolk.

95 *Above* Cobbles at Trunch, Norfolk.

4
A New Order

CHANGE IS TOO MYSTERIOUS, too subtle, to be measured by date. A slowly altering view of life, a shift of emphasis from the religious to the secular, had been manifest in countless ways during the 16th and 17th centuries, not the least of them the sharp decline in church building and the florescence of a domestic architecture which owed less and less to ecclesiastical influence and inclined more and more to the classical horizontal mode which was so perfectly attuned to the serene and confident philosophy of Locke and Shaftesbury, the new understanding of Nature's laws and the exhilarating sense of liberation from the darkness and barbarism of the Gothic past which this engendered. Even the humble farmhouse and cottage were affected by the prevailing habit of mind, and there is plenty of evidence, as the reader will have noticed, of a growing awareness of the changing outlook in the farming practices of the 17th century. The transformation of the English landscape and of methods of farming which went forward so energetically under the Hanoverians was but the continuation of a process set in motion by the scientific advances of the previous age.

When Daniel Defoe was riding through Britain at the beginning of the 18th century he saw great tracts of land, millions of acres, still farmed on the open field system, and desolate moors and heaths of vast extent even in such gentle counties as Surrey, Berkshire and Hampshire. He describes cottagers, yeoman farmers and craftsmen pursuing their traditional ways of living, working and cultivating the fields under the peculiarly favourable conditions created by enterprising middlemen who were finding new markets for farm produce.

But a number of reasons were conspiring to quicken the pace of the revolution already under way. The population of the country was mounting – it more than doubled between 1700 and the reign of George IV, from about $5\frac{1}{2}$ to over 11 million – and a larger proportion of it than ever before was concentrated in the towns. The traditional way of increasing the food supply by reclaiming new farmland from forest and fen, moor and mountain, was far from exhausted, as Defoe's account shows, but it was realized that inevitably the day would come when the ancient remedy could not be applied. It was wholly in key with the temper of the age, eager, experimental and inquiring, preoccupied with physical science and the phenomena of nature, that a solution should be sought in developing the new methods of tillage and breeding which the most enterprising farmers

Opposite
96 High House Farm, Bawdsey, Suffolk.

127

had already adopted, methods dictated by a scientific approach to agriculture. This approach was encouraged by a spate of publications on the subject, many of them written by practising farmers, such as Jethro Tull (inventor of the seed-drill, for more effective sowing), William Ellis, William Marshal (author of *The Landed Property of England* and of detailed, lively studies of rural economy in different counties and regions of England), and the prolific Arthur Young, agricultural reformer, traveller and journalist. Enthusiasm for farming became a cult embraced by great landowners and small squires alike. It was symptomatic of the vogue that George III wished to be known as 'Farmer George' and that he contributed to Young's periodical, *Annals of Agriculture*, under the name of Ralph Robinson.

The possibilities for growing new and better crops and for improved techniques could only be realized through enclosure and the creation of rationally planned, compact farmsteads under the firm control of the individual owner or manager. So a procedure which had been localized and sporadic became an all-embracing national policy carried forward by Acts of Parliament which multiplied from only 8 before 1714 to as many as 1,768 by the end of the century. More than 700 further Acts were passed after the General Enclosure Act of 1845 and even after than date there were more than a further hundred awards of the right to enclose.

The counties most severely affected by enclosure were parts of Lincolnshire and Rutland, Bedfordshire, Huntingdonshire, Northamptonshire and south Cambridgeshire, Oxfordshire, Warwickshire, parts of Berkshire, Gloucestershire and Derbyshire, and the East Riding of Yorkshire. In the pastoral hills of the far north and the south-west and in those regions such as Kent, Essex, Suffolk and Somerset where enclosure had begun early, the agrarian revolution made but a mild impact. But over a great area, especially in the Midlands, mazy landscapes of narrow strip cultivation, winding tracks and green lanes were turned into chequerboard patterns consisting of large, approximately square, hedged fields with straight, grass-verged roads running through them. The hedges had a ditch on one or other side of them; unlike the hedges of ancient enclosure, where many varieties of trees and shrubs flourished, they were always of hawthorn, interspersed occasionally with ash trees and elms and sometimes – in Cambridgeshire and the small area of Suffolk which had not previously been enclosed – with holly. In much of the limestone country, over part of 97 Yorkshire and conspicuously in Derbyshire, stone walls took the place of hedges, netting the land in a taut mesh of glittering rock fragments. In Northamptonshire thorn trees, now grown to giant size, spring here and there with magical effect from the stone walls.

This wholesale ordering of the countryside domesticated, tamed, it. It came near to realizing Addison's tentative suggestion that an entire estate, including the cornfields and meadows, might be made into a kind of garden; and while in the open country nature was subdued by enclosure, the formal gardens of earlier times, paradisian symmetrical plots walled against the dangerous chaos of wild nature, were thrown open to merge with the surrounding fields, and instead of formality the contrived irregularity of cave and precipice, lake and waterfall, trees and glades conjured up images of nature's more savage aspects without their physical hazard.

Professor Hoskins speaks of the Northamptonshire poet John Clare's poignant sense of loss when the woods, heaths and fields of his native Helpston were enclosed in about 1820, and of his rage against the 'improvers':

> Inclosure, thou'rt a curse upon the land
> And tasteless was the wretch who thy existence planned.

But only half a century later Richard Jefferies in Wiltshire wrote that nothing he had read of or seen equalled the beauty and delight of English fields and meadows, and he marvelled at the variety of birds rejoicing 'in the plenty of the hedgerows'. And the crowning touch in George Eliot's marvellous picture of the Warwickshire countryside at the beginning of *Felix Holt* (1866) is her description of the hedgerows:

> Perhaps they were white with May, or starred with pale pink dogroses; perhaps the urchins were already nutting among them, or gathering the plenteous crabs. It was worth the journey only to see the hedgerows, the liberal homes of unmarketable beauty – of the purple-blossomed, ruby-berried nightshade, of the wild convolvulus climbing and spreading in tendrilled strength till it made a great curtain of pale-green hearts and white trumpets, of the many-tubed honeysuckle which, in its most delicate fragrance, hid a charm more subtle and penetrating than beauty. Even if it were winter the hedgerows showed their coral, the scarlet haws, the deep-crimson hips, with lingering brown leaves to make a resting place for the jewels of the hoar-frost.

Before the recent destruction of many of these hedges the sight of the May landscape over a great part of England was the thrilling climax of all the visual pleasures of spring: the whole terrain, farm and cottage, church and village were embowered in a foam of blossom which everywhere filled the air with its heavy scent.

The results of enclosure for many cottagers have often been described. The rural labourer had been wont to supplement his wages by keeping livestock on the wastes; now these rights were largely lost, with a consequent accentuation of the problem of poverty. The fact that by the end of the 18th century more than £7 million were levied in taxes for Poor Rate, while taxations for other purposes amounted to only £1½ million, speaks for itself. The situation was made worse by the Law of Settlement which had been passed in 1662 to make each parish responsible for its own poor. It meant that a man who wished to qualify for relief had to remain in his own parish. When the numbers of paupers began to increase parishes made every effort to get rid of them; some landlords even allowed cottages to decay so that the inmates were forced to seek accommodation outside the parish. The parish they had left then became 'closed', a place where no Poor Rates were levied because there were no longer any poor. The needy were thus gradually driven into the 'open' parishes where Poor Rates were high. The confrontation lasted until long after the Poor Law Reform Act of 1834, which abolished 'outdoor relief' – the payment of subsidies from the parish rates to people who remained in their cottages – and made life in the workhouse deliberately harsher. After the rise in prices towards the end of the 18th century the lot of those living in open parishes might be utter destitution and starvation. A labourer, his wife and two children were found dead in a house on the village green of Datchworth in Hertfordshire in 1769, and in the same year four other labourers of that parish died of hunger.

The contrast between the records of such tragedies and the descriptions in the literature of the period of the more than ample fare served in some farmhouses – the delicious mutton, venison and veal, poultry and game, cream and cheese, ham and bacon, fruits and vegetables, all from his own farm, with which Smollett's Matthew Bramble, squire and farmer of Brambleton Hall, loaded his table; the 'fine Tench (taken out of my pond in the yard) stewed, a Rump of Beef boiled, and a Goose rosted, and a Pudding', which was one of the more modest of the dinners Parson Woodforde (1740–1803) describes in his *Diary of a Country Parson* – is symbolic of the gulf which had begun to develop between farmers and their workers, and which was to become unbridgeable. The old community life of the farmhouse was already disrupted: unmarried workers still lived in the house, though as J.C. Loudon observed in his *Encyclopaedia of Agriculture* (1825), 'sleeping rooms for unmarried farm servants, in most parts of Britain, are generally such as to merit extreme reprobation'. But maids and men no longer sat at table with the family: they ate apart at a scrubbed wooden table while the farmer and his family dined at a table spread with a snowy cloth. Successful farmers were putting on airs. William Cobbett, who rode and wrote about England a hundred years later than Defoe, indignantly criticized a farmhouse that boasted a parlour (which differed from the parlour of the 16th and 17th centuries in that it was used only for sitting), 'aye, and a *carpet* and *bell-pull* too'. And the poet Crabbe's Farmer Ellis had 'a superior room' graced by books and prints, and his wife was 'beyond our station clad' in fashionable dresses from the town.

Yet not all farmers prospered under the new system. Small farmers seldom owned the land they cultivated and when the landlord decided to amalgamate several farms, a frequent occurrence because large estates were more suited to the new agricultural methods, the tenants were squeezed out of existence. Cobbett gives graphic accounts of what was happening in the early years of the 19th century. 'The farmhouses have been growing fewer and fewer', he writes of Windsor Forest; in Wiltshire, 'only about 8 manor houses survive from an original 50 or more'; in the parish of Burghclere in Hampshire,

> one single farmer holds by lease, under Lord Carnarvon, as one farm, the lands that men now living can remember to have formed fourteen farms. In some instances, these small farmhouses and homesteads are completely gone; in others the house is gone, leaving the barn for use as a barn or as a cattle shed; in others the outbuildings are gone, and the house, with rotten thatch, broken windows, rotten door-sills, and all threatening to fall, remains as a dwelling of a half-starved and ragged family of labourers, the grandchildren, perhaps, of the decent family of small farmers that formerly lived happily in this very house.

For the practical farmer enclosure meant that in grazing country cattle and sheep could be moved from one field to another so that they were always feeding on freshly springing grass; and in corn country the more general use of root crops and clover improved the system of rotation: instead of a bare fallow following two corn crops, two corn crops were now separated by a crop of roots and a crop of clover. The new root crops, which were planted in exact rows by Jethro Tull's drill, enabled farmers to keep more animals and to nourish them during the winter. The annual slaughter of livestock was abolished, inferior stock could be weeded out and the breeder could encourage the most desirable traits in cattle, pigs and sheep. The winter fattening process was accelerated by the discovery during the 18th century of a new protein-rich food, oilcake, a by-product of the oil-seed crushing industry.

The adjective 'improved' resounds through the abundant livestock literature of the period and the names of breeders such as Robert Bakewell, John Ellman, Mr Fowler of Rollright and the Colling brothers became famous all over the country. The lively portraiture of prize cows, bulls, pigs and sheep – pictures like James Ward's *The Durham White Ox*, John Boultbee's *Portrait of a Ram of the New Leicestershire Kind* and Thomas Bewick's *Remarkable Kyloe Ox* – testifies to the breeder's success and records

97 The landscape of enclosure – Haworth Moor, Yorkshire.

131

the gross forms of the 'improved' animals. But they were not gross in the eyes of those who bred or those who painted them: Bewick found the principles of beauty and utility united and exalted in 'the quality of the flesh and its propensity to fatness'. In his *History of Quadrupeds* (1789) he describes the transformation of the old longhorn cattle achieved by 'the late Mr Bakewell' with the help of cows of the 'Cauley breed' produced by Mr Webster in the Trent valley, and an engraving exhibits the short spindly legs, tiny head and fat loins and quarters of the remodelled beast. Juxtaposed engravings invite us to scorn the original black-faced muscular ram of north-west Yorkshire and the old long-legged, large-headed Teeswater breed of sheep, and wax enthusiastic over the bloated, improved ram and the monster of obesity, weighing 'sixty two pounds ten ounces per quarter avoirdupois' produced by Bakewell's method. That method was crowned with signal success in the case of the Holstein or Dutch breed of cattle: an ox fed by Mr Hall of Whitley, Northumberland, weighed 187 stones, 5 pounds. Together with a small-headed, similarly 'improved' cow it gazes complacently across Bewick's page to the artist's triumphant account of the beauty of its 'fattening quality' and its early fitness for the butcher.

The new farms created out of hitherto unused waste in this adventurous period were not all by any means made at the expense of cottagers and squatters. The celebrated examples of Holkham and the neighbouring country are cases in point. Arthur Young describes north Norfolk before enclosure as 'a rabbit and rye country', a landscape of 'boundless wilds and uncultivated wastes inhabited by scarce anything but sheep'. Enclosure and the fertilizing of the sandy topsoil with the underlying marl metamorphosed this barren prospect into an incomparable vista of rich cornfields punctuated by new farmhouses and cottages. Exmoor in Devon was a treeless unpeopled expanse, though cottagers in open villages on its fringes grazed their livestock upon it. They were each given a piece of land while 10,000 acres were bought from the Crown by John Knight, a manufacturer from the Midlands, who, after an heroic struggle going on for more than thirty years, enclosed it, introduced lime to increase the fertility of the soil and established seventeen thriving farms to which he and his son gave eloquent names – Honeymead, Cloven Rocks, Wintershead, Red Deer, Tom's Hill and Larkbarrow.

62 There had always been such solitary farmsteads in upland grazing country: Fellfoot Farm at the foot of Wrynose Pass in Westmorland is an instance. Now, with the coming of enclosure on a nationwide scale, farmhouses in predominantly corn-growing regions were also built far from the village, isolated with their cluster of outbuildings in fields where no habitation had yet been seen, for farmers needed to be close to their hedged lands where new experiments were being tried out. Odstone Farm, near Ashbury in Berkshire, is such a case: the house, with attic windows recalling the farm servants who once slept in the dormitories they lit, stands prick-eared alongside the systematically arranged barns, granaries, stables, cowbyre, piggeries and carthouses. A greater emphasis on shelter reflects the larger number of beasts that were reared and retained by the improved methods.

Another farm, at West Burton in Lincolnshire, gives a clearer image of the concentration of the Georgian farmyard and its importance. It was in the yard that the manure upon which the new farming so greatly depended was accumulated, not haphazardly in the manner of previous centuries, but scientifically. The straw from the harvest went straight into the yard; the hay and the root crops fed the animals in the stock buildings and then, out of those buildings and into the yard came the manure which, trampled into the straw by the cattle, was made ready for the fields.

The little walled front garden of the farmhouse, with its gate opening immediately from the fields onto a path leading to the main entrance, which is never used, is a special and endearing feature of 18th- and 19th-century farmsteads of the enclosures. Here the farmer's wife could grow a few flowers away from all the business of the farm going on at the rear of the house. Not that she did not have her own domain there as well, for close to the back door lived the poultry and the pigs which, feeding as they mainly did on left-overs from the house and dairy, were her special responsibility. Pigs, which had still occasionally been permitted to forage in the woods in Stuart times, were now everywhere kept in sties 'as near as may be', as Young wrote, with little runs in front of them. And so they continued to be housed until the introduction of scientifically controlled, prefabricated, mechanized and windowless fattening houses of modern industrial farming in the late 1960s.

The other and major concern of the farmer's wife was the dairy, which at the West Burton farm occupied the projection at the back of the house. The propinquity on the farm of dairy, pigs and poultry is remarked by the Suffolk author of *The Farmer's Boy*, Robert Bloomfield, whose Giles, returning from the fields, finds

98 Farmstead at West Burton, Lincolnshire.

133

The clatt'ring Dairy Maid immersed in steam
Singing and scrubbing midst her milk and cream,

and cannot hear her speak

For pigs and ducks and turkies throng the door
And sitting hens, for instant war prepared.

So high was the value set on the farm dairy in the Georgian period that farmers were granted exemption from the Window Tax for this room, provided that it was labelled 'DAIRY' or 'CHEESE ROOM' and barred with wood or iron. Professor Barley mentions a farmhouse at East Coker in Somerset which in 1961 still had the word 'DAIRY' painted above one of the windows.

When new farmsteads were built out in the fields, old village farmhouses and sometimes the adjacent barns were often divided into two or more cottages, a process which has already been noticed. But not all farmers found it necessary to move from the village and many farmhouses can be seen confronting the street to this day with the remnants of their barns and outhouses clustered alongside or behind them – particularly, of course, in lands of earlier enclosure. Newton Farm, at Kewstoke in Somerset, built in 1710, went on operating as a farm right up until the last decade. In the north and in Devonshire farmsteads based on the traditional long-house design were still being built in villages at the end of the 18th century, and some northern villages, such as Milburn in Westmorland, consist wholly of little farms of long-house type built in the 18th and 19th centuries.

A small farm created on the east Sussex downs some three miles from Glynde by early 19th-century Parliamentary enclosure was actually planned to be managed from a farmhouse in the village, an arrangement which endured until 1970. Furlongs was a mixed farm combining corn-growing with cattle and sheep breeding. A pair of flint cottages set at the end of a long straight track originally housed a shepherd and a cowman, while open-fronted shelter sheds, a granary and a barn were ranged about three sides of a yard at the rear. Deserted now except during the lambing season, for the modern farmworker refuses to accept either their remoteness or their primitive inconvenience, these cottages stare with their blank windows from a tangle of brambles, nettles and knobbly apple trees to the far distant gate at the end of the chalky track.

Occasionally cottages which were built before enclosure can be seen thus stranded amid fields far from a road. Such cottages accentuate the complex and intimately co-ordinated harmonies of some of Constable's paintings of the Suffolk landscape, and a pair of ochre-coloured, half-timbered, steep-roofed little houses, one thatched, the other with its former thatch replaced by tiles, rise from a meadow of flowering grasses in the shadow of ash, elm and oak at Worlingworth Green. Their isolation is as much due to the Parliamentary commissioners as that of the Glynde cottages, for they mark the edge of a former common before it was enclosed.

Even if the Glynde farmer did not move from the village, his yard out in the fields corresponded closely to the description of the standardized plans which a report issued in 1814 by the Board of Agriculture (founded twenty

99 Open-fronted animal
shelter at Manor Farm,
Thornton Steward,
Yorkshire.

years earlier through the exertions of farming landowners) assumes to be
those of all farmsteads 'where improvements have taken place': 'a main
body or corn barn having a tangent wing at each end for stables, cow tyes,
open sheds, etc., the yard opening to the milder points, the south or the
south east'. And such numbers of farmsteads of the period do conform to
this plan that the statement of the Board seems on the whole justified. The
quadrangular yard was not new, but it was now regularized. A fine and
compact example is Manor Farm at Thornton Steward, on the borders of
north and east Yorkshire. There had been a farm on the site since the early
Middle Ages, but at about the time of Trafalgar much of it was rebuilt to
conform to up-to-date principles. The new three-sided foldyard is of local
stone with open arcaded animal shelters, a barn, hayloft and fattening
house; and while it is eminently practical it is nobly proportioned and
reveals a new awareness of the visual possibilities of such utilitarian
buildings. A farmstead near Holme in east Yorkshire, Aggthorpe Hall
Farm, though a less complete interpretation of the standard plan, is
informed with a pronounced sense of design. The range incorporating the
stables, a granary and hayloft, brick-built and pantiled, at once catches the
eye, for it is perfectly symmetrical, marked by a tower-like central bay
suggestive of Palladian influence and articulated by restrained mouldings
and decorative ovals, while the openings are based on the forms of lunettes
and Venetian windows.

99

100,
101

Similar buildings appeared fairly frequently in the recently enclosed regions of east Yorkshire and Lincolnshire, and it was natural that they should house the stables: the horse had always enjoyed rather better quarters than other farm animals and now when horses were kept not only for fieldwork but for riding and fox hunting, the sport which more than any other fired the imagination and enthusiasm of every class of countryman, stables became an important architectural feature of the great country house and were often of distinguished design on the farm. The obstacles created by enclosure in the form of hedges and ditches seem to have encouraged rather than deterred the huntsmen, according to William Somerville in *The Chace* (1735):

> They strain to lead the field, top the barr'd gate,
> O'er the deep ditch exulting bound and brush
> The thorny-twining hedge.

Though the farmyard at Aggthorpe Hall Farm does not quite correspond to the quadrangle of the textbooks, it does include a magnificent barn filling the range opposite the stables. It follows the traditional plan of three bays with a central door opening onto the threshing floor, and the timber roof embodies the king-post design long favoured in Yorkshire; yet the interior is more suggestive of the spirit of ancient Rome than many a grand mansion built at that time to the precepts of Vitruvius: the proportions are of antique dignity and the classical affinity is enhanced by the plain arched openings giving onto a single aisle and by the colour and texture of the reddish brown, speckled brick.

Local farmers and builders were made aware of new elements in the design of farm buildings through plans and elevations which appeared in some of the books on the latest techniques of farming which have already been mentioned. Marshall gives a full account of the steading he built on his farm near Croydon, Surrey, in 1771, with lively references to the local carpenters who carried out the work, and offers it 'as a mirror in which others may see the advantages and disadvantages of their own farmeries'. Young reproduces plans for farms and farm buildings in his *Farmer's Guide in Hiring and Stocking Farms* (1770), pointing out the necessity for ample shelter for cows, carts and implements and for a layout concentrating the farmer's labours and facilitating the effective production of the all-important dung, but also stressing the importance of attention to 'symmetry and appearance'. C. Waistell, whose *Designs for Agricultural Buildings* appeared posthumously in 1827, at the end of the period of agrarian reform, has this to say about the style of farm buildings: 'Being intended solely for the purpose of utility, they should be simple in their forms and perfectly plain . . . to utility alone everything else in agriculture must be subordinate.' Yet Waistell's plans testify as eloquently as any other product of the age to its remarkable concern for aesthetics. His ranges are perfectly symmetrical. They are often fronted with blank or open arcading in the classical style, and the upper walls of his barns and granaries are sometimes adorned with ornamental roundels and ovals. In one design a barn planned to house the threshing machine (invented by the millwright Andrew Meikle in 1786) stands high between an arcaded haystore and

100
101

Opposite
100, 101 Aggthorpe Hall Farm, near Holme, Yorkshire: stables, granary and hayloft, and interior of the barn.

identical shed for the ox-driven gear propelling the machine; it has a central arched opening framed by pilasters, with blank arches on either side. The whole composition might be part of some great house, and the plan in which it is incorporated recalls that of the Roman villa-farm.

While the simplest elements of classical design in no way conflicted with the practical purposes of farm buildings, the trimmings of the Picturesque and Gothick taste might be outrageously inappropriate. Yet such was the influence of the taste of the day that even Marshall cautiously recommended a decorative, polygonal farmyard; and Loudon, an experienced farmer as well as a sensitive artist, the author of the remodelling of Great Tew, Oxfordshire, and of its enchanting setting, suggested extravagant Italian and Gothick styles for some of the farm buildings shown in his massive *Encyclopaedia of Cottage, Farm and Villa Architecture* (1833). Other writers – for the most part architects with no connection with farming addressing themselves to aristocratic and wealthy patrons – give greater rein to fancy and conceive of the farm as a picturesque incident in a landscaped estate. In his *Fermes Ornées or Rural Improvements* of 1800, John Plaw, for instance, looks upon farm buildings as 'calculated for landscape and picturesque effects' rather than as food-producing units. He describes a farmhouse as an object to be seen from a gentleman's mansion and presents one design for 'A farmyard having the Appearance of a Monastery', an idea which the courtyard layout of the Georgian farm might quite readily suggest, though Plaw views it as a cluster of towers and turrets which, 'embosomed with stately trees, give an air of antiquity, consequence and grandeur, which would form a leading feature on an estate of considerable extent'. In his book of plans for 'Cottage Farms' (1805) Joseph Gandy mentions the traditional half-timbered building in tones of horror, as exhibiting 'all the deformities of the timbers': he includes drawings for farm buildings in a comparatively sober classical style, but they are nonetheless decorative rather than convenient. Among them is a huge circular dovecote, surmounted by a cupola and weathervane, a pleasing object but one which was unlikely to take shape on any of the new working farmsteads since pigeons were no longer indispensable for the addition of variety to the winter diet. W. Barber designed an octagonal farmyard in the Grecian manner, and Robert Lugar drew up plans for a farmhouse and farm buildings in the 'Old English Style', a picturesque version of traditional thatch and 'brick, stone or lath and plaster, as most convenient for the situation'.

Although Arthur Young saw a great ambitiously and ornamentally designed semi-circular piggery in Sussex, and at least one great landowner rejoiced in a Dairy 'in the Chinese Taste', fantasies like those of Plaw and Lugar had little impact on farm buildings. Their considerable effect on the farmhouse itself and on the cottage will be considered in the next chapter. Judging from Lugar's remarks, his picturesque plans might have been carried out by local craftsmen using local materials. But many of the designs illustrated in Loudon's *Encyclopaedia* demanded the skills of professional surveyors and engineers. This was significant for times to come, but for the moment local workmen with their traditional skills were still able to erect farm buildings that met the new requirements and to

XII

102 *Above* Granary over a cartshed, and from right to left cowhouse, stable and open-fronted shelter at Painsthorpe, Yorkshire. The materials are brick, limestone and pantiles.

103 *Below left* Barn with a hay storage loft, Little Barrington, Oxfordshire.

104 *Below right* Granary, hayloft and cowbyre at Gnaton, Devon.

Opposite
XI Corrugated iron
cottage at Bawdsey,
Suffolk, its design derived
from the hall-house
(compare Pl. II).

translate textbook designs into their own idiom. Village craftsmen, for example, built the model fattening house for oxen which Young saw at Retford, Nottinghamshire, in 1771; and local builders in the hop-growing areas of the southern counties constructed and equipped the oast houses which were becoming more and more numerous and which changed their shape during this period from the rectangular design of Flemish origin to the circular. Flues from enclosed iron stoves rose all round the inner walls to the conical roof, discharging smoke and fumes through a chimney furnished with a pivoting cowl (at first made of wood, later of metal) painted white, shining against the sky above the pippin red of the tiled roof and brick cylinder.

It is interesting that the textbook writers either specify local materials for the realization of their designs or make no reference to the subject, taking the use of traditional resources for granted. In most districts, even when the layout of a new farm might be of the standardized pattern, the buildings themselves were scarcely distinguishable from those of the 16th and 17th centuries. Cobbett does not record any particularly modern buildings, and indeed many of the farms he saw had remained quite untouched by the improved system of farming: old-fashioned implements were still being used, threshing with the flail was the custom, and seed was sown broadcast in the biblical way. In the Cotswolds and along a great part of the limestone belt the vernacular style which had crystallized during the 17th century was preserved with only the most superficial changes, and a late 18th-century barn at Little Barrington in Gloucestershire hardly differs from those of the previous two hundred years except in the poorer quality of the roof timbers. A granite and slatestone group at Gnaton in Devon, where cowbyre and hayloft are aligned with the farmhouse although separately roofed, maintains all the traditions of the region, and shows the influence of contemporary taste only in the simple formality of the design, the ordered openings and low-pitched roof. It is the huge expansion of unbroken wall space and its wonderful texture which, unselfconsciously exploited by the village stonemason, gives such distinction to the buildings. The multi-sized pieces of granite and splinters of slatestone, softened and delicately stained by the weather, varying in tone from silver grey to moss brown, look as though held in a mesh and make a background like a deep etching for the red Devon cows in the yard and the swallows pitching up and down in their season. An 18th-century barn at Wimpole, Cambridgeshire, built of timber on a brick base with a thatched roof, discloses its date by the use of iron nuts and bolts in the carpentry, but it remains a traditional barn and is seen at once as an attenuated, aisleless version of the medieval masterpiece at Great Coxwell.

The fashion for brick, which is such a conspicuous mark of the period, is as evident in farm buildings as in farmhouses and cottages, and it is brick structures on the farm – such as those at Aggthorpe Hall – which most often display innovations in style. But again, though perhaps more neatly and conveniently ordered than they might have been a hundred years earlier, there are many groups of 18th- and early 19th-century brick-built farm buildings in which a 17th-century farmer would encounter nothing unfamiliar. Local limestone and brick are combined in such a group at

103
104

10

100

Painsthorpe, Yorkshire. The granary above the cart shed contains sufficient space for the storage of two harvests, an innovation suggested by Young, and the cowhouse adjoining it is provided with chain ties, divisions between the animals and up-to-date sloping standings; but it is as ill lit and low as the one at Hawkshead.

One new building did make its appearance on the 18th-century farmstead and might have seemed strange to a farmer of an earlier period. The threshing machine, which took the form of a drum fitted with pegs and revolving within a concave casing, was powered by steam as early as 1804 on a Norfolk farm visited by Young. This was exceptional: where it was used the threshing machine was generally horse-driven and on some farms, especially in the north, where it was known as the 'gin gang', a small circular, polygonal or occasionally rectangular building was sometimes set next to the barn door like an ecclesiastical side chapel or chapter house, to shelter the horse and the driving gear. The gin gang might be open, the king-post roof resting on stone pillars, as at Blencarn in Cumberland, or the intervals between the piers might be boarded, as in the brick and pantile example at Howden in Yorkshire. Another structure which was mentioned for the first time in the 18th century – by a Swedish traveller, Pehr Kalm, who saw an example in Hertfordshire in 1748 – was a thatched timber skeleton built out in the open fields to give protection to carts and implements. Such structures were probably traditional, for an exactly similar ephemeral shelter was constructed in Essex at Clay Wall Farm, Steeple Bumpstead, some thirty years ago with the most primitive type of flat roof formed of rough saplings laid like joists across the timber frame and heaped with straw. Another such structure at Bloys Farm in the same parish was used as storage for hay and itself looked just like a haystack. It served much the same purpose as the Dutch barn, and may have inspired that Victorian innovation; though unlike the prefabricated metallic open barn it took its place naturally in the landscape.

*   *   *

The urge towards symmetry and order which underlay 18th-century farmstead plans animated the design of farmhouse and cottage as strongly and in general more effectively, for the appearance of the vernacular house suffered a change as vital as that which turned the hall-house with cross-wings into a rectangular block. The façade at Toseland is an early instance of the desire to achieve a rational, balanced disposition of doors and windows, and Ufford's Hall at Fressingfield, built in the late 17th century with a central entrance and tall panelled chimneys at either end, is another. But the gabled individualism of these houses could not now be tolerated by any farmer or landowner who knew anything of fashion. The domestic front, whatever happened behind, must now be designed in the terms of a classical order, the proportions of the floors ideally conforming to those of an antique column. Through the medium of books and prints far exceeding in number those concerned with farm buildings, specifically addressed, very often, to masons, joiners, carpenters and bricklayers and published at prices within the reach of most craftsmen and farmers, this strange notion,

105, 107

106

71

which could only have been so eagerly accepted because it corresponded to a deeply felt attitude of mind, penetrated the most remote rural areas.

Among the few books owned by Arthur Partridge, tenant farmer of Shelley Hall in west Suffolk, at the time of his death in 1789 was William Halfpenny's *Twelve Beautiful Designs for Farmhouses*. Halfpenny, who himself started out as a carpenter, was one of a stream of authors of pattern books which followed on Moxon's pioneer *Mechanick Exercise* published in 1682. Halfpenny's most popular production was *Magnum in Parvo: or The Marrow of Architecture*, a practical handbook on the classical orders which appeared in 1725; while his *Art of Sound Building* informed the local builder how to set out brick arches, niches, columns and pilasters in the Doric, Ionic, Tuscan and Corinthian styles. Isaac Ware's *Compleat Body of Architecture* (1756), dealing thoroughly with the use of the orders, with proportion and ornament and with materials, sites and foundations, must have meant uphill work for the craftsman reader of the mid-18th-century village, yet it was studied to such effect that a doorcase with an open pediment and rounded fanlight shown by Ware materializes again and again, with slight variations, on farmhouse façades all over the country. Francis Price's *British Carpenter* went into four editions and then there were Batty Langley's many titles, the most widely read architectural textbooks of the time, the best known of which were probably *The City and Country Builder's and Workman's Treasury of Design* (1740) and *The Builder's Jewel* (1741). With the aid of these and many similar publications master carpenters, bricklayers and masons were inspired to produce the multitude of enchanting small symmetrical houses and cottages which enrich English country towns and English villages and grace the fields of enclosure.

Despite the dissemination over all parts of the country of pattern-book designs farmhouses and cottages were still being built in the vernacular styles. New cottages of stone and thatch in the Northamptonshire village of Ashby St Ledgers sustain the tradition already established there in every detail except that they are uniform and are furnished with the simple form of the sash window which, moving sideways and thus dispensing with weights, was ideally suited to low cottage walls. In the north, as at Whashton, in the North Riding of Yorkshire, one-storeyed dwellings continued to be erected according to old local usage.

Even when the orders were fully adopted by country craftsmen vernacular building had not come to an end: the new vision, at least before the spread of standardized, mass-produced materials, was absorbed into the vernacular. There is rarely anything stereotyped or academic about a farmhouse or cottage in the Georgian style. A feature taken from a pattern book invariably turns out to be more than an imitation of the model. The interpretations of the doorcase just mentioned, for instance, each bear the impress of the carpenter's individuality in the rendering of proportions, pilasters, door-head and panelling. And as long as bricks were not mechanically produced and were fashioned of local clays, their popularity constituted no more than a minor threat to the close relationship between house and soil, and extended rather than diminished the scope of the country builder. Brick and white-painted wood are the materials most readily associated with the period; and the ways in which local craftsmen

105, 107 *Top and above* Gin gangs, housing the horse-driven gear to power a threshing machine in the barn, at Howden, Yorkshire, and Blencarn, Cumberland.

106 *Left* Roughly constructed open thatched shelter, Clay Wall Farm, Steeple Bumpstead, Essex.

with the traditions of medieval carpentry and of those wonderful Tudor chimneystacks behind them translated the vocabulary of classical architecture into brick and wood are a source of delight in all the country towns and villages of south and south-east England. There was no form of classical ornament – modillions under the eaves, capitals, complicated mouldings, decorated keystones and swags of fruit – which was beyond the skill of brickworker and carpenter. The choicest refinements are generally found in houses built for the wealthier landowners and for the increased number of professional men and gentry with little connection with the land who were now living in the country; but countless smaller farmhouses either newly built or refronted in brick from the early 18th century onwards abound in ingenious and rustic adaptions of textbook examples which reconcile a formal design and classical embellishments with their setting.

Sometimes a farmhouse design corresponds so closely to the pattern-book prototype that the effect in the landscape can be startling. The formidably plain expanse of the academically correct quoinless façade of the second half of the 18th century appears with hardly any distinguishing details at both Foulden in Norfolk and Bawdsey in Suffolk. The very name High House comments on the unexpectedness in remote farming country of a tall building of urban aspect rising through three floors: High House Farm, Bawdsey, is indeed a remarkable sight in the flat lonely fields, beside a lonelier shore, of the strip of east Suffolk between Orford Ness and the mouth of the Deben. The Foulden farm is just anchored to its foundations by the vermilion colour of its local brick and its shining pantiled roof. The wall of flint cobbles separating High House Farm from the road establishes its region. Here the touch of the local carpenter gives life to the doorhead,

96

where a small white-painted pediment sits whimsically on top of the fanlight within the enclosing broken pediment of the doorcase; and the sober grey-brown bricks of the front and the paler, silvery grey bricks of the window heads were locally made. These window heads, so quiet and unobtrusive, bear triumphant witness to the brickmaker's art, for the finely jointed, wedge-shaped bricks have been most delicately cut and gauged to resemble pleating.

The window heads of two-storeyed Red House Farm, Withersdale Street, also in east Suffolk, display similar careful jointing and pleat effects and may perhaps be the work of the same craftsman. This house, like that at Bawdsey, consists of a new fashionable block set across the gable end of an older farmhouse. Here the local bricks are of a clear light red with a stronger colour for the big parapet which is dotted with vitrified headers and half conceals the roof of pantiles. The doorway is an elongated version of the design followed at Bawdsey; screen walls on either side of the façade, each adorned with a pineapple and pierced by an arched opening, create an illusion of country-house wings, while the Palladian ideal is further brought to the notice of the passing villager by simple ball-topped piers.

At Bretforton in Worcestershire and at Much Wenlock in Shropshire, the abrupt height of brick-fronted additions to earlier buildings and the eccentricities of the designs attract the eye to farmhouses standing a little distance from the road behind hayfields. At Much Wenlock a band of pallid

109 One-storeyed stone and pantiled cottages, Whashton, Yorkshire.

110 An older farmhouse refronted at Bretforton, Worcestershire.

111 A former hall-house transformed at Little Common, Hooe, Sussex.

stone divides the dark brick façade exactly in two, so that the upper half with its exceptionally tall side chimneys looks like a separate house which could be lifted from the ground floor and put down elsewhere. The triple windows of the ground and first floors at Bretforton and the central, arched window of the first floor are of grotesque aspect. Emphatic blocks of local masonry ray out against the brickwork, aping in stone Adam's device of fanfilling over the Venetian window but omitting the order framing the light.

For all the subtleties and oddities of handling which link them to their environment – and closer study would doubtless reveal many more localized details – the relationship between houses such as these and the traditional farmhouses and cottages of earlier centuries is distant. But when the building materials are wholly those of old tradition, a symmetrical façade and a pilastered, pedimented porch readily become part of the vernacular and of the landscape; and sometimes, when the adjustment of the old-fashioned to the modish is only partial (as it so often is in the case of houses built just before or just after 1700), the actual process of the absorption of the new by the old can be watched.

111   A unique transformation of the traditional into the Georgian idiom occurs at Hooe in Sussex, where the front of a vernacular farmhouse was brought into line and furnished with a central, pilastered and panelled porch and a balanced arrangement of sash windows. Yet it remains un-classical: the roof of the former hall block still inclines steeply, the eaves line is not continuous, and the former cross-wings are marked by a rise in the height of the modish parapet. White-painted woodwork conspicuously outlines the whole composition, and a complete covering of the timber frame above the brick base with russet tiles accentuates the individuality of this encounter and fusion of the old and the new.

112   At Slough Farm, Acton, Suffolk, a cross-wing has been left in position and fashionable alteration has been concentrated on the former hall block. It has been extended at the front to form a new two-storeyed house with a balanced façade. At the rear the roof still slopes at its original steep angle

and with the jutting cross-wing covers the kitchen, dairy and former brewhouse. The profile is one which is met with again and again in both farmhouse and cottage. This was one way in which the rural builder could adjust the foursquare plan of the pattern books to the traditional farmhouse: the outshot was made as wide as the main rooms and consisted of two service rooms, while in front were the hall and parlour. Even when the farmhouse conforms outwardly to the foursquare plan and looks as though it might be the very replica of Barton Cottage as described by Jane Austen within, it may well have come by this shape in the course of the natural development of the vernacular plan: the sloping extension at the rear may have been raised to the height of the front in answer to the continual and general desire for more and improved accommodation. This is indeed what seems to have happened at Moat Farm, Great Tey, Essex, which stands on a long inhabited site, for the large external chimneystack serves only the front half of the house.

The characteristic 'double-pile' (two-rooms deep) plan of the Georgian house does occur rather more frequently that I seem to have suggested, though it is usually found in much larger and grander farmhouses than humble Great Tey, and the instances are often Victorian. Professor Barley saw examples of the Hanoverian period in Nottinghamshire, and the houses at Odstone and West Burton described earlier incorporate the plan.

Moat Farm, timber-framed and washed pale ochre, and Slough Farm, which differs from the traditional Office Farm at Methwold only in the height and symmetrical arrangement of its front wall, could not be anywhere but in East Anglia. At Stoke-by-Clare a more imposing but equally eloquent example of the Georgian style in Suffolk dress blandly regards the fields of which it is the focus. With walls of small, glistening flints, both rough and knapped, with yellow brick quoins and window heads, a parapet of variegated yellow brick, brick stringcourses and vertical rows of alternating single headers and stretchers marking the bays and flanking the windows, Flint House quaintly suggests the elements of Palladian articulation in two dimensions.

112 A new symmetrical front added to an old timber-framed and flint farmhouse at Acton, Suffolk. The projections on either side of the chimneystack contain a bread oven and a side oven.

113 The Georgian style in local flint dress at Stoke-by-Clare, Suffolk.

IX

98

112
56

113

149

114 Boarded cottage at Goudhurst, Kent, its door copied from Isaac Ware's *Compleat Body of Architecture* (1756).

Timber-framed, clapboarded cottages have already been encountered. In Essex, east Hertfordshire and Kent, where the half-timbered style had flourished with exceptional vigour, timber frames were still popular even though often now of imported deal. They assumed the current rectangular shape with studs closely set to carry an outer covering of weatherboarding, plaster or tiles. The translation of the Georgian style into any of these mediums enhances the intimate, homely character of the traditional idiom and invests both farmhouse and cottage with a toy-like charm. But when symmetry is manifest in an overdress completely of wood the resulting doll's house is always irresistible, whether it be faded and neglected with bow windows on either side of a correctly proportioned and elaborate door emerging from a thicket of bay and berberis, brambles and convolvulus, as at Goudhurst; whether the carpenter has exaggerated the element of make-believe by curiously grooving the weatherboarding to simulate stone, as on a farm façade at Tenterden; or whether it stands precariously, its single lateral chimney only just balanced by an outshot on the opposite side, as at Cranbrook, or sits firmly and trimly at the end of a garden path, its white paint and horizontal lines set off by a blaze of flowers and the glowing red of chimneystacks and roof tiles, as at Sissinghurst.

The classical influence in cottages such as these last two is no more than skin deep. The builders of many a humble cottage and many a modest farmhouse came no nearer to pattern-book examples of the Georgian style than the creation of an impression of symmetry, combined with a rustic version of the sash window and the merest attempt at a classical doorcase. The carpenter at Great Tey was content with just the suggestion of a simple pediment. At Poynton Green in Shropshire, the square panels of the traditional black-and-white house of the district take a reluctantly

Opposite
115 Clapboard at Sissinghurst, Kent.

rectangular, balanced shape with a central porch on spiralling supports more suited to a four-poster bed than a door. A stone cottage at Arncliffe and a stone farmhouse near Thackholme, both in Yorkshire, a slate-stone mill house at Lerryn, Cornwall, for all that it rises through three floors, and the farms and cottages on the green at Ravensworth, again in Yorkshire, all speak the language of their region far more distinctly than the vocabulary of Palladianism.

Where the long-house was indigenous the farmer's quarters might now exhibit an orderly disposition of door and windows in an otherwise scarcely changed exterior, as at Milburn in Westmorland, or in Cornwall at a farm near the Fowey River and in a farmstead of slate-hung cob at Warbstow, where the shippen later became part of the house.

Not only is the rendering of the classical ideal delightfully eccentric and sketchy on the façades of innumerable farmhouses and cottages but very often the door is not precisely in the middle. At Arncliffe and Poynton Green, in some of the cottages at Ravensworth and in a refronted former farmhouse at Cranbrook, the entrance only approximates to the central position. The door of a cottage at Manningtree is directly in line with the chimney, which remained in its traditional position when the façade was Georgianized, and just inside the door is a small lobby set against the jamb of the fireplace, an arrangement frequently found in plans deriving from the hall-house and of course controlling the position of the door. At Cranbrook and Arncliffe, where the chimneys are at the gable ends, placed thus to leave ample room for the staircase, as was normal in houses of two or more storeys built after the beginning of the 18th century, the door has been pushed considerably to one side to give greater length to the parlour, and this disposition also harks back to the hall-house plan. At Cranbrook the parlour opens from a passage (now called the hall) which preserves the position of the old screens passage, while at Arncliffe the front door leads directly into a corner of the kitchen. At Poynton Green the plan, though not quite symmetrical, is of the foursquare type with four rooms on each of the two floors, the front two on the ground floor consisting of the living room to the right and the little-used parlour to the left, the kitchen and former dairy at the rear with the staircase between them.

Our knowledge of the appearance of farmhouses and cottages from about 1700 onwards is augmented by pictures and prints and also by the reports of the many travellers encouraged by the improvements of roads and waterways. Between the accession of Queen Anne and 1750 more than four hundred Road Acts were passed and during the second half of the 18th century more than sixteen hundred were passed. Travellers less well known than Marshall, Young and Cobbett, among them Charles Vancouver who wrote of Hampshire farms, William Stevenson who journeyed through Dorset, William James and Charles Malcolm who wrote memoirs of a tour in Sussex, Alexander Dennis who gives an illuminating account of rural life in Devonshire, John Bailey who recorded what he saw in Durham, and William Hutchinson who kept a diary of his experiences in the north, confirm the evidence provided by surviving farmhouses and cottages that traditional materials were everywhere being used despite the widespread infiltration of brick and the substitution in some areas of tiles for thatch.

Opposite
116 Local tradition – stone slates, walls of rough mountain stone, the house distinguished from its outbuildings by a coat of whitewash – is stronger in this little farmstead at Arncliffe, Yorkshire, than Georgian influence.

117 A converted long-house of cob, slate-hung, at Warbstow, Cornwall. The upper window on the left was once the opening into a hayloft.

Such writers sometimes give glimpses of internal structure too, which add background detail to the information provided by probate inventories. John Bailey saw single-storeyed cottages in Durham which exactly resembled those at Whashton mentioned earlier; they generally consisted of but one room measuring about 15 by 16 feet in which the cottager and his family lived, while another smaller room housed a cow, tools and coal. New stone cottages in Northamptonshire are praised by William Marshall for their large living rooms and two bedrooms. Earth and brick floors were common in the Midlands and over much of the south-east; stone-flagged floors were encountered in the north, the south-west and the Cotswolds. Dennis saw floors of cobblestones in Devon kitchens and dairies as well as floors of plaster which were made from lime, coal ashes, loamy clay and horse dung. Pehr Kalm speaks of upper floors in the farmhouses of Essex and Hertfordshire constructed of imported deal. Farmhouse parlours in many districts were boarded with oak or elm. Walls in larger farmhouses, like The Grange, Yattendon, might be panelled, or wainscotted, but in general they were limewashed. Wall-paintings and wall-cloths were no longer fashionable, and although colour-printed wallpapers were available from the mid 18th century only the richest farmers hung them in their parlours. But Crabbe's Farmer Ellis, it will be remembered, furnished his walls with prints, and framed paintings sometimes appeared in the homes of well-to-do farmers. Theophilus Lingard of Writtle, who died in 1744, had two pictures in his parlour and twenty prints in frames on the stairs. Gilpin saw prints on cottage walls in 1777 and observed that some cottagers had pasted 'ballads on the wall with good effect'.

The fashionable dalliance with the Rococo in great houses and town mansions, a well-controlled reaction against the severe regularity of the orders, had little influence on farmhouse interiors, though the extraordinary instance of its introduction into the modest farmhouse at Belton, Suffolk, known as Browston Hall must not be overlooked. A wholly unpretentious exterior conceals a riot of scrolly and free figurative plasterwork. A huge eagle hovers uncertainly above the staircase and in the parlour a sun face beams from the midst of symbolic representations of the Four Ages of Woman, strong featured heads in medallions, and above a unique, shallow relief of wonderful spontaneity shows a shepherdess and her swain, lovers trysting, and a man and woman standing on a promontory in a high wind gazing across a river to a little mill, while at the top of the picture a pennon waves from a towered house.

Several travellers noticed stores of coal in both farmhouse and cottage. Thomas Pennant remarked in 1782 that because of the development of canals and the deepening of navigable rivers 'places which rarely knew the use of coal are plentifully supplied with that essential article'. The effects of Theophilus Lingard almost forty years earlier already included 'coal racks, a pair of iron cheeks, fender, shovel, tongs and poker'. The new fuel supplemented the traditional farmhouse and cottage faggots, logs, furze and turf; and where coal was used dog grates (with dogs, firebacks and bars all united), and occasionally the elegant basket of polished steel, replaced the open fireplace with its firedogs; and later on the dog grates gave way to fixed cast-iron grates which filled the whole of the recess and assumed a

variety of forms. The famous Carron Foundry, with extensive warehouses in London as well as in Scotland, opened in 1759 and was soon followed by foundries in Glasgow, Birmingham and Manchester; and standardized grates, stoves, fenders and ironmongery of all kinds slowly found their way into country homes from the last quarter of the 18th century onwards. A local craftsman would occasionally create his own version of one of the fashionable grates: the best bedroom at Harthill Hall Farm, Alport, is 156 furnished with a pleasingly crude imitation of the double ogee hob grate with cheeks made of roughly hewn stone.

But in a great many unassuming farmhouses and most cottages, as inventory lists of fireside implements and accessories show, the fire was still laid on the open hearth, and firedogs, firebacks, chimney cranes, iron pots, skillets and pipkins were as prominent as ever they were. Some hearths were furnished with floors of iron plates raised on brickwork at each side to leave an open space under the hottest part of the fire, which could be used for baking and for keeping food hot. Such an arrangement was still in daily use in the kitchen of Frog's Hall, a farm near Biddenden, Kent, in 1953. Dr 119 Pococke in his *Travels through England* (1750) says that in the West Country bread was baked under an earthenware pot placed on top of the iron plate.

118 Rococo plasterwork of the parlour ceiling in Browston Hall, Belton, Suffolk.

The parlour fireplace of the grander farmhouse might be a Palladian composition with an opening framed in a classical order and with the cornice exaggerated to form a mantelshelf. It might well be the work of the village carpenter or mason working with the aid of a pattern book, but by the end of the reign of George III it was more often than not ordered from London or from the county town. The two-storeyed compositions seen in the houses of landowners, professional men and gentry living in the country – the 'continuous chimneypieces' such as those at Langleys at Great Waltham or Peckover House at Wisbech – seldom grace the tenant farmhouse. The chimneypiece most generally found in farmhouse parlours had side pilasters with consoles under the cornice like the one in the present drawing room at Newbourn Hall, Suffolk. Varied by individual details and enrichments, it remained popular throughout the 18th century and for most of the 19th. The rustic cottage version, which persisted until well into the present century, was a tall, plain rectangular opening with a mantelshelf supported by stout consoles or brackets. The chimneypiece of Mrs 153 Holman's cottage at Crewkerne represents a design which had been repeated with little diversity in cottage after cottage all over the country for almost two centuries. Just below the mantelshelf there usually hung, on a rod, a valence to increase the draught. Theophilus Lingard owned such a rod and valence, and valences are shown in 18th-century paintings of cottage interiors – in Morland's *Cottage Fireside*, for instance. The valence was still commonly seen in cottage homes of the mid-20th century, and Mrs 120 Tye's living room at Little Barrington displays a freshly laundered one of faded pale blue rep.

We have already come across some of the books of Arthur Partridge, a Suffolk farmer. Just as the fine libraries of the great country houses and the modest libraries of country gentlemen like Jane Austen's Mr Bennet testified to the remarkable literary civilization of Hanoverian England, so the books owned by many tenant farmers bear witness to a vigorous interest in reading. In addition to Halfpenny's volume of farmhouse designs, Partridge owned Foxe's *Book of Martyrs*, Gerard's *Herbal* of 1579, the *Spectacle de la Nature*, *The Guardian* in two volumes, several historical works, and the '*Dictionarium Rusticum and Urbanicum*', a farming and household encyclopaedia published in 1704. An Essex farmer of Great Wigborough who died at the end of the 18th century left historical, topographical and technical books together with an English dictionary, the Bible and *Tristram Shandy*.

Judging from inventories very little of the fine and lighter mahogany furniture we associate with the Georgian period found its way into the farmhouse and cottage. But the remarkable number of pieces, especially chairs of the late 18th and early 19th centuries, which have survived show with what zest and humour and originality and with what piquant touches of personality the village cabinetmaker interpreted the achievements of the great furniture designers, again from pattern books, in elm, beech and oak. His chairs prance, stamp or stand sturdily and heavily inert with hearts or flowers cut out of their splats; their backs may turn into ribbon fretting (catching the spirit but never the letter of Chippendale), or they may be adorned with twisted plaiting emulating in wood the straw plaiting of the

119 *Below* The hearth in the living room at Frog's Hall, Biddenden, Kent.

120 *Right* Mrs Tye in her living room, Little Barrington, Oxfordshire.

corn dolly maker. Ladder-back and spindle-back chairs were the country craftsman's particular invention, and of these there were endless individual varieties. Theophilus Lingard owned six such chairs, as well as a 'cane couch and squab'. The chair seats were of the same rustic rushes which were still the principal source of light in farmhouse and cottage, as they had been in Tudor times. Traditional iron rushlight holders occur as frequently in 18th-century inventories as tea kettles and teapots. Tea, brought to England by the East India Company, was drunk in large quantities by all classes, and even John Piper, a pauper of Bottisham, Cambridgeshire, whose goods were listed when he asked for poor relief in 1782, owned two teapots and a tea kettle.

Theophilus Lingard also included amongst his possessions a piece of furniture which is not mentioned in inventories of earlier than 18th-century date – the farmhouse dresser. It stood in his pantry where it was resplendent with fifty-five pieces of 'Delph and earthenware', sixteen pewter plates and two small dishes. The dresser in its early form was a long narrow table with drawers upon which food was 'dressed' for the pot, and had only recently developed into a feature fitted with drawers and cupboards below and with shelves above it displaying plates and dishes.

5
Rustic Homes for Rural Labourers

THE ORIGINAL LIVING QUARTERS of the little long-house at Warbstow 117
visited in the last chapter are lit not by sash windows but by casements with
pointed lights in the Gothic style. Venetian windows with ogee-shaped
central lights and a straight-headed porch on spiralling posts invest an
ochre-coloured, timber-framed farmhouse near Portchester, Hampshire,
with exotic charm and piquancy. A porch at Bibury, Gloucestershire, of 125
grey limestone mottled with black-spotted raw siena coloured lichen, set
on Ionic columns with a scrolling ogee pediment adorned with delicately
carved paterae and with the name 'IVY COTTAGE' in rustic lettering, brings a
breath of the enchanted palaces of Thomas and William Daniell's *Oriental
Scenery* to this Cotswold village. At Wylye, Wiltshire, a jaunty little stone 123
front sports upper bull's eyes ingeniously made from cart wheels and
pointed openings like the tops of lancets on either side of a Gothic door
shaded by a pert canopy. Not even an ugly cement rendering can destroy
the alert, cheerful air imparted to the long plain façade of a pebble and
pantiled cottage at Knapton, Norfolk, by five identical small pointed 124
windows widely and symmetrically disposed above and on either side of a
pointed door with Gothic panels. Huge cusped and pointed windows
overwhelm the diminutive front of Chapel Cottage at West Bradley,
Somerset, and, with the crocketted panel carved with a Paschal Lamb over
the door, parody the medieval domestic style, conspicuous in this area,
favoured by Abbot Selwood. At Court Farm, Damerham, in Hampshire, 122
actual 14th-century stone-mullioned windows look irrationally from a
balanced, pedimented façade.

These and countless other spirited, unselfconscious rural echoes of
Horace Walpole's Strawberry Hill Gothic, perhaps in some instances
sparked off by a pattern book (for several of the writers who instructed
country craftsmen in the art of Palladian design included in their manuals
examples in the Gothic style), constitute no more of a threat to the
vernacular tradition than the wholly classical composition. Village builders
responded with energy and wit to the fashionable demand for a mimic
revival of the style which had first nourished their traditional skills. Their
approach to both Gothic trappings and medieval fragments was as
spontaneous, untrammelled and confident as that of the Yorkshire farmer
who built a severely classical house at the end of the ruined arcade of
Coverham Abbey, which happened to stand on his land, and set Purbeck
marble effigies of cross-legged knights in alarming, upright positions in the
farmyard wall. Earlier in these pages it was suggested that the symmetrical
square or rectangular farmhouse might be seen as a natural development of

Opposite
121 Milton Abbas,
Dorset, a planned
Picturesque village of
local cob and thatch set in
a contrived landscape (see
p. 170).

122 *Above left* Court Farm, Damerham, Hampshire. 123 *Above right* Wylye, Wiltshire.
124 *Below* Knapton, Norfolk. 125 *Opposite* Bibury, Gloucestershire.

126 Rectory Farm, Winterborne Came, Dorset.

127 Late 18th-century model cottage at Finchingfield, Essex, built by a local squire.

the hall-house plan, and so long as local materials were used ties with the past and with place were strong enough to withstand the addition of a few mock Gothic ornaments. The hint of artificiality they bring with them is all the more attractive because it speaks the language of *Northanger Abbey*, the authentic language still of 18th-century sanity and moderation.

The real danger to vernacular tradition as well as to classical form rose from the absorption of the taste for the Gothic into the cult of the Picturesque. The cottage at Chippenham in Wiltshire, once rural, called Bagatelle, exhales a suspicion of what this might mean. The rough dark limestone of its walls, laid with the minimum of mortar, the pallor of the deliberately rudimentary stone porch and large-scale Gothic details magnify the effect of its Lilliputian size. Almost as fantastic a play upon the traditional image of the cottage and outshot as the folly Convent-in-the-Wood at Stourhead, it is as consciously rustic, a cottage conforming to an unreal dream of rural life.

Just such a stage-like view of rusticity, though generally more inflated than this, determines the appearance of all those circular, square, rectangular or polygonal, extravagantly thatched miniature cottages and occasional farmhouses, some with ostentatiously rustic porches, others with flamboyant bargeboards or with wide eaves held up by slender columns, which embellish park scenery and roadsides in every part of England. Neat, irresistibly pretty compositions such as the rectory 126 farmhouse at Winterborne Came in Dorset, with its tall thatched roof and pannier-shaped thatched verandahs; the beguiling little lodge at Wantisden, Suffolk, a single low storey topped by tea-cosy thatch gathered into a tall central chimney and with a pointed door in the middle of its tiny 127 front; a minute thatched and plastered hexagon at Finchingfield in Essex, with black-painted hoodmoulds above the porch door and Gothic lattices, prototype of the pottery cottages made a little later in Staffordshire; the

lodge at Mendham, Suffolk, with three dwarf bays divided by fragments of columns from Mendham Priory and with a big finial sprouting from its central gable – they are all enchanting, but about them, however faintly, clings that air of reverie and escapism present also in much of the literature of the period, which was eventually utterly to pervade and destroy the vernacular tradition.

The dwellings I have just mentioned are carried out in local materials – Winterborne Came in Dorset cob and thatch, the Wantisden and Mendham lodges in flint, the Finchingfield hexagon in plaster over a timber frame – but they are not so much the village craftsman's version of a fashionable novelty as the correct realization of a drawing or plan by a professional designer, like those published in W.F. Pocock's *Architectural Designs for Rustic Cottages, Picturesque Dwellings, etc.* (1807) or in Charles Middleton's *Picturesque and Architectural Views for Cottages, Farmhouses, Villas, etc.* (1802). A lodge at Hainton, Lincolnshire, built of brick with a roof of the Welsh slates which the new canals were bringing to many inland counties by the end of the 18th century, exactly corresponds to a model cottage shown in Loudon's *Encyclopaedia*, of which he says: 'Though no marked features of any style appear in this elevation, yet it must be acknowledged to exhibit something more than the mere expression of purpose; because it would be equally, and to all appearance, as much a human dwelling, without the columns as with them.' There could hardly be a conception more removed from that which animated the cottages and farmhouses briefly described at the beginning of this chapter. The lodge unites classical and Tudor elements with remotely oriental overtones. The very way in which the slates are laid is as much an affront to local tradition as their origin, for instead of being arranged in diminishing courses they are all the same size, the exact number having been calculated and ordered through an agent from the distant Welsh quarries.

129 The Tattingstone
Wonder – cottages
masquerading as a church,
at Tattingstone, Suffolk,
1760 – seen from the rear.

The cast-iron casements at Winterborne Came, delightfully decorative
though they are, represent a similar alien intrusion in the rural craftsman's domain, for they were mass-produced. Their counterparts and
innumerable variations on the theme can be seen everywhere in buildings
of widely different 19th-century dates, for instance in rows of cottages at
Horsham, Sussex; Hawley, Hampshire; Calmsden, Gloucestershire (in the
windows of otherwise typical Cotswold cottages); and in the Victorian
brick lodge at Stratton Park, Hampshire, where the startling whiteness of
the window filigree is matched by that of vigorously looping and
undulating bargeboards and prominent finials, while roughcast quoins
stripe every projection including those of a shallow, hugely castellated bay
window. Arresting, aggressive even, this outlandishly patterned, fancy-
dress cottage bears high-spirited witness to the opposition between the
Picturesque and the traditional and has as little connection with its setting
as the lodge at Hainton. As the Rev. Samuel Jackson Pratt exclaimed in his
Cottage Pictures, as early as 1790,

128

> Farmhouse and farm too are in deep disgrace
> 'Tis now the lodge, the cottage and the place!
> Or if a farm, ferme ornée is the phrase
> And if a cottage, of these modern days
> Expect no more to see the straw built shed
> But a fantastic villa in its stead.

But Picturesque architecture could go to greater lengths than this. The
furniture of the landscape garden, the sham ruins and the follies, moved out
into the surrounding countryside to form part of pictorial compositions

which extended far beyond the domain of the big house. Tenants of Squire White at Tattingstone, Suffolk, were housed in three cottages disguised as a church tower and nave; a Gloucestershire cottager at Cerney Wick was given a round tower pierced by Gothic lights; a cottage covered with bark was considered suitable for a forester; the new toll cottages, usually round or polygonal, sometimes took the form of toy castles, like the fat little fortress, white with a black outline, which once transfigured the main road near Hungerford in Berkshire; and it was thought appropriate that the door of the village smithy should be framed in a giant horseshoe, as it is at Tinwell, Leicestershire (though the smithy has now become the post office).

The most practical men were not immune from the prevailing craze for ruins and for the sublime and fearful aspects of Nature. Arthur Young, that passionate advocate of agricultural reform, so eager when touring Britain to point out the merits of enclosure and the benefits of the latest methods of fertilizing the land and breeding livestock, describes Duncombe Park in Yorkshire and the ruins of nearby Rievaulx Abbey in terms worthy of that apostle of the Picturesque, Dr Gilpin. He cares nothing for the style or detail or even the history of the ruins but with a shiver of delight extols 'the broken, rugged and terrible' aspects of the remains 'half seen from a distance, for thus the imagination has a free space to range in, and sketches ruins in idea far beyond the boldest stroke of reality'. It was a Surrey farmer who, according to an *Essay on Design in Gardening* by George Mason, had

129

130 Cinder Hall, Little Walden, Essex.

131 Detail of the sham ruin masking the front of The Jungle, Eagle, Lincolnshire.

132 Random carstone at Wells, Norfolk.

first thought of making his domain part of an 'Elysian scene'. In about 1768 Philip Southcote enclosed his farmstead at Chertsey and the surrounding meadows and cornfields with a belt of trees in which he established a menagerie and built a Gothic temple. Fifty years later, when enthusiasm for the Picturesque had become frenzy, another farmer, Samuel Russell Collett, who also had a menagerie and for this reason called his farm The Jungle, turned his Georgian house at Eagle, Lincolnshire, into the
131 semblance of a fantastic, rugged Gothic ruin merging into the landscape and achieving just that vague, indeterminate character which Young admired. The true front of the farmhouse is entirely masked by a castle disguise with a square tower at one end, a semi-circular turret at the other and a bastion-like projection in the middle. But it is a castle in the process of dissolution: its outlines are blurred by the gnarled confusion of the masonry, the roughness of purple-red bricks and huge clinkers laid this way and that in wild disorder, and by the clutching arborescence of ancient ivy, scarcely distinguishable from the curving oak boughs from which the openings, crudely and uncertainly Gothic, are fashioned. Another
130 farmhouse, one front of which masquerades as a corbel-turreted castellated tower house, exhibits the same predilection for rough unconventional materials. It confronts the road near Little Walden, Essex, its flint and brick façade electrifying the landscape with a dazzling display of fleur-de-lys and pendant lozenge and ball shapes, mock machicolations and quoins, all carried out in black clinker on a silvery flint ground, and a clinker frieze decorated with squares and diamonds outlined in pebbles. The Jungle and Cinder Hall belong to the world of folly and fairy tale, and
132 so does a tiny cottage at Wells-next-the-Sea in Norfolk: its carstone fabric is in mad disarray and the absence of a balancing window on the ground floor of a near symmetrical façade gives singular edge to the voice of unreason.

Conceits such as these sprang from an attitude very different from that which gave rise to Slough Farm at Acton or High House at Bawdsey. '*Je sens donc je suis*' had taken the place of '*Cogito ergo sum*'; and the cultivated sensibility for Picturesque effects was allied to a new and fashionable interest in rustic life and in the cottager as well as the cottage. The cottager's humble dwelling was the inspiration for the rural retreats from the hurry of town life which, as the architect Edmund Bartell observed in 1804, made 'pleasing objects in the landscape'. Like his cottage the cottager himself represented that earlier, simpler form of existence in which it was believed true happiness lay. A series of treatises, poems, novels and plays exalted the natural over the civilized man, the primitive over the sophisticated, the rustic over the urban. Cowper celebrated the health and wholesomeness which dwelt among the poor; Wordsworth preferred the homely truths of children and rustics to the utterances of philosophers; Thomas Day and Mrs Inchbald found virtue in the cottage, vice in the palace; Nathaniel Kent, author of one of the earliest pattern books to include plans for farm labourers' cottages (*Hints to Gentlemen of Landed Property*, 1775), thought that 'cottagers are indisputably the most beneficient race of people we have'.

Views such as these, disastrously mistaken though they have proved to be, were sometimes, of course, associated with dismay at the actual conditions in which many cottagers were living. John Wood the Younger of Bath recoiled with horror at some of the sights he encountered in Somerset in 1792 – 'shattered, dirty, inconvenient, miserable hovels, scarcely affording a shelter fit for the beasts of the forest'; and Thomas Davis, the steward at Longleat in Wiltshire, in a pamphlet about the housing of farm labourers addressed to 'the Landholders of this Kingdom' and published in 1795, protests that 'Humanity shudders at the idea of the industrious labourer with a wife and five or six children being obliged to live or rather exist, in a wretched, damp, gloomy room of 10 or 12 ft. square, and without a floor; but common decency must revolt at considering that over this wretched apartment there is only one chamber to hold all the miserable beds of the miserable family.'

But if benevolence prompted the building of some of the many new cottages dating from the period of agrarian revolution onwards, there were other motives quite apart from the widely enjoyed pleasure of indulging in the Picturesque for emotional and aesthetic reasons. The landlords of enclosed fields, particularly when several farmsteads had been amalgamated, were unable to get labour without providing cottages for the married men. The desired 'closed' parish, where no Poor Rates could be levied forcing landowners to support the local poor, could sometimes be created by building a new village with exactly the required number of cottages. In the 'open' villages parish officials were putting up cottages of the cheapest local material, like those seen at Whashton, while squatters continued to live in ephemeral huts they had built themselves or to occupy makeshift homes in derelict buildings. H. P. Wyndham, one of the stream of late 18th-century topographical writers, saw a number of families living wretchedly in the stables of a house at Seagrove on the Isle of Wight which had never been completed. The cottagers in the 'closed' village might live

133 Model cottages in the village of Houghton, Norfolk, 1729.

rent-free but they were entirely in the hands of the landlord. 'They've allus got to do just what they be told, or out they goes, neck and crop, bag and baggage' – as, a century later, Flora Thompson heard the labourers of Lark Rise, an open hamlet in Oxfordshire, say disparagingly of those who lived in estate cottages.

133   The very idea of the planned village is a negation of traditional development. One of the first to be built, Houghton, designed for Sir Robert Walpole's tenants in 1729 perhaps by his agent and built by the men employed in the estate yard, has as little connection with the typical Norfolk village as the ubiquitous group of modern council houses. Rows of austere paired cottages line the road leading up to Houghton Hall. At its gates stand two farmhouses, one with a raised, pedimented central bay, and a row of one-storeyed almshouses. All the buildings are of whitewashed brick, tenuously linked to their setting only by their pantiled roofs. The pairs of cottages, which are not always identical but which together make up a square plan, bear no relation to traditional paired cottages; and except that, because of their early date, they have no Picturesque trappings, they prefigure the suburban semi-detached convention. But with their large gardens and well-proportioned, if small, rooms, they provided cottagers with homes which beside such miserable hovels as those seen by Wood and Thomas Davis must have seemed utopian. They were a good deal better even than some of the romantic cottages built later as rustic landscape ornaments: one of the lodges at Audley End in Essex, of brick with pretty flint panels, a Gothic porch and a fine, ornate Tudor chimney, consisted of but two minute ground-floor rooms, one of which contained the stair, and one upper room – and it was the home of a family of six.

Yet though the accommodation might sometimes be excellent the 18th-century planned village, designed by a well-known architect for a landlord with aesthetic interests but not much feeling for the vernacular, was not always congenial to the cottagers and could diverge more widely from the evolutionary path of rural building than Houghton. A traveller passing through Lowther, Westmorland, in 1802 described it as half empty and neglected, and it was as desolate more than a hundred and fifty years later. Designed for Lord Lonsdale perhaps by James Adam, it is based on 18th-century urban concepts and was to have taken the form of Greek crosses opening from either end of a circus. The village was never completed: today a crescent of one-storeyed dwellings flanked by two-storeyed houses, and one side of one of the Greek crosses made up of one- and two-storeyed cottages, stand bleakly in open, remote country. Not even the use of local stone for walls and roof can bring them into harmony with the older farm buildings and cottages of the region. Harewood in Yorkshire, planned as a terraced street leading up to the park gates of Harewood House by John Carr of York for Edwin Lascelles at about the same time as Lowther village, presents a similarly urban, alien face to its surroundings, a beautiful ridge of country above the Wharfe.

Ripley, also in Yorkshire, begun in 1827 but completed only in 1854, affords as great a contrast to the truly vernacular theme. The texture of the terraced cottages is rougher than at Harewood. Some of them are gabled, and the windows are filled with Gothic lights and surmounted by Tudor dripmoulds, introducing a light touch of fantasy to the strictly ordered layout which is confirmed by the mock medieval cross in the middle of the little square to which the terraced street leads. It is a toy theatre image despite the robust character of the cottages, and a toy theatre town rather than a village. Then suddenly with the intrusion into the street in 1854 of the extraordinarily inappropriate town hall gentle dalliance with Gothic trimmings explodes into heavy Picturesque caprice. With its ornate stepped gables and finial-chimney, its battlemented turret and buttressed bay and huge mock Perpendicular windows, the town hall dominates the village and imbues it with that unreal atmosphere so often engendered by the Picturesque attitude.

The planned village offered such obvious opportunities to the amateur of the rustic and the Picturesque that it is surprising to find one such village at least which is not an architectural exercise and where rusticity is not emphasized, the Picturesque is not consciously sought and tradition is upheld. Blanchland, Northumberland, built on the site of an abbey in the mid-18th century by the trustees of the Crewe estate, about whom little is known, follows the ancient pattern of many villages in the eastern coastal counties above the Thames, for it consists of an open space with the cottages built in terraces about its perimeter – just as the Anglo-Saxon settlers built their dwellings close together about such a space as the best means of defence in a region vulnerable to attack. The professional architect had nothing to do with Blanchland. The cottages, of roughly hewn big blocks of sandstone from the Fells, were built by village masons. They are not identical, and fragments of the monastery fabric appear in some of the walls, or in the structure of a door or a window; now and then the remains are more than fragments, and a mysterious stone recess or a curious passage may give a Gothic air to a little interior, though never with a hint of sophisticated contrivance. Seen from afar the village, lying in a wooded fold of the high moors, sinks into the natural landscape, wholly at one with it. Audley End village too, a row of plastered timber-framed dormered cottages with an irregular roof line, proclaims the idiom of its region, Essex, with no more than a suspicion of conscious striving after Picturesque effects.

121   The case of Milton Abbas in Dorset is different. The cottages – perhaps designed by the great Sir William Chambers, who remodelled the Abbey – take the same semi-detached form as those at Houghton, though they are much smaller: each contains only four rooms. The pairs are set like the Houghton cottages in straight rows in a disciplined rhythm not found in traditional villages, though the cob and thatch of which they are fashioned does relate them to the soil. But what distinguishes this village from Houghton or Blanchland, Ripley or Lowther is that it has been imagined and planned as part of an artificially created landscape composition. Milton Abbas was so sited by Capability Brown for Joseph Damer, later Earl of Dorchester, that together with the perfectly placed lake and the carefully planted valley and enveloping hills it made a living picture. The cottagers, like the inhabitants of other planned villages, Nuneham Courtenay in Oxfordshire, for instance, and Wimpole in Cambridgeshire, had been moved from their original homes in the interests both of Picturesque layout and the creation of a closed village.

At Great Tew, as I have already mentioned, Loudon successfully fused the old and the new, traditional and planned rusticity in a design which perfectly realizes Sir Uvedale Price's formula for the Picturesque village: it is characterized by variety in outline and texture, the cottages are scattered about little irregular greens on an uneven terrain, the colour of the Cotswold stone is just 'of that rich, mellow, harmonious kind so much enjoyed by painters', climbing plants twine about porches and flourish in warm angles and crannies, and the whole composition is brought into deep luxuriant harmony by tree planting. It is the forest of giant evergreens and great chestnuts crowding the sloping site, plunging the village into verdant shade, which more than the delicately Picturesque details – the two-storeyed porch with a Gothic arch and curvilinear bargeboards added to a 17th-century cottage, the hooded, latticed casements, the sinuous eaves line of steep thatch – gives substance to the sense that Great Tew is a lost domain into which one has stumbled by chance, hardly of the same world as nearby Nether Worton or Sandford St Martin. Loudon's village, like his *Encyclopaedia*, when considered in relation to his other manifold interests and activities, is as revealing of the power of contemporary taste as Arthur Young's transports over Picturesque scenery. At the time, 1809, Loudon was managing the estate of Great Tew Park and setting up an experimental farm on the most advanced scientific lines. If when entering Loudon's village we are aware of contrivance, we are not conscious of a single jarring note: the planner's aesthetic intervention heightens the charm of the Cotswold vernacular and the danger to tradition inherent in the Picturesque is held in check.

XII

The threat declares itself openly in the group of estate cottages known as Blaise Hamlet, near Bristol, which John Nash designed only a year later for the Quaker banker John Harford of Blaise Castle House. Nine cottages disposed at random about a shaven lawn and an off-centre sundial on a tall stone shaft evoke a stage image of the village and the green, a concentrated display of rough contrasting textures, unbridled irregularity and extravagant rusticity. The cottages are constructed of local rubble, but the traditional method of laying the stones with the biggest at the bottom has been abandoned in favour of the rugged and the anomalous. Tall red brick chimneys, clustered or single, round, rectangular and star-shaped, start from the tiles, heavy stone slates or bulging thatch of the roofs; gross finials ornament the gables, one of which takes the form of a weatherboarded dovecote while a plastered cove sweeps forward from another. The miniature scale of both the green and the hamlet, the delightful vegetation – hollyhocks and old cabbage roses smothering latticed casements, wisteria and clematis and honeysuckle trailing over crazy stonework – and the profound tranquillity of the place, despite the fact that it is now encompassed on three sides by suburban development, all conspire to engender a sense of timeless well being. Yet viewed in the context of vernacular tradition these cottages and their setting come no nearer to it than the sentimental, nebulous Christmas card cottage.

134 Cottage in the Picturesque Blaise Hamlet, near Bristol, Somerset, designed by John Nash in 1810.

A like Picturesque and hazy conception of traditional cottage architecture gave rise to the village of Old Warden in Bedfordshire, built from about 1830 onwards for Lord Ongley. Shadowed like Great Tew by dark evergreen trees, terraces of thatched cottages display caricatures of the Bedfordshire thatcher's semi-circular dormers, while the walls are roughcast and here and there overlaid with struts simulating the appearance of half-timber, and the doors are framed in trellis porches. Trellis work, though one of the most unfailingly pleasurable of Picturesque inventions, conveys no feeling of place. Like the ornamental bargeboard it did however offer wonderful scope for the skill and imagination of the village carpenter; the infinite variety of design, the grace and zest with which Gothic and classical motifs in every kind of combination have been translated into airy fretwork, delight the eye in almost every region, whether the trellis redeems a plain façade or enhances the attractions of a 'cottage ornée'.

The elephantine heaviness which, in a climate of growing uncertainty, soon overtook the theme formulated at Blaise is seen in a peculiarly grotesque form in a group of estate cottages at Sudbourne, Suffolk. The alarming rapidity of industrial growth and its social consequences emphasized the differences between urban and rural life. At the same time, the increase in the number of landlords who derived their income from commercial enterprises rather than farming, and the incipient threat contained in the Reform Bill of 1832 to the social system with which English agriculture had always been associated, created an atmosphere of deep unease which was reflected in a monstrous intensification of Picturesque affectation – particularly, as might be expected, in the design of estate cottages. Every roof at Sudbourne is enveloped in the thickest thatch, embellished with every ornamental device in the thatcher's repertoire and often sweeping to within a few feet of the ground. Steep gables supported by coarse brackets jut forward over every door and ground-floor window, thrusting dormers break every roof line. Massive bargeboards, lofty chimneys of diverse shape, rough tree trunks, interlacing twigs and bogus half-timber all manifest a vulgar fancy-dress view of rusticity while announcing the death of the true vernacular.

At Sudbourne, bloated and obscured though they are, the basic components are recognizable as derivatives of English rural architecture. But the habit of assembling elements suggestive of various regional characteristics had already expanded to embrace themes from distant lands. Loudon's *Encyclopaedia* showed eclectic designs and he had included details of porches and campaniles in the Italian manner, and the architect J. Thomson, author of *Retreats* (1827), recommended a Grecian cottage, a Corinthian villa and an eccentric 'Irregular House' which boasted an Italianate tower, a colonnade and a rotunda as suitable additions to village architecture. P.F. Robinson, who had made drawings for farmyards and cowbyres in the Swiss and Italian styles, designed a whole village in the Picturesque mode for which the 'scenic drawing' showed fanciful half-timber alongside Norman arcading, Cotswold and Tuscan details and a Moorish verandah; and he also drew up plans for cottages which were Grecian, Swiss, Palladian, Elizabethan and Tuscan in character.

Ingredients such as these went into the extraordinary mixture which became the Derbyshire village of Edensor when it was removed from its original unacceptable site in full view of Chatsworth in 1839 and rebuilt on the edge of the park in a setting of beeches and hills laid out by the great gardener Joseph Paxton (who was later to design the Crystal Palace). The cottages masquerading as pretentious villas were planned by John Robertson, an architect from Derby. Local stone can do little here to reconcile these houses with the landscape. North Italian, Romanesque, Gothic and Tudor motifs mingle in a single building; rustic porches are furnished with obelisks, spiralling chimneys and scrolled bargeboards consort with ball-topped piers, a castellated entrance lodge looks towards a Lombardic tower and a Swiss chalet adorned with a Georgian pediment. Yet the fantasy is lifeless, all the early Picturesque enthusiasm and gaiety have evaporated: this is escapism in earnest, a pedantic association of themes from every architectural source which never becomes a vital whole.

Fortunately the international eclecticism of Edensor had no more than a minor influence on later farm and cottage building: the village was essentially a precursor of urban villa development. But estate cottages continued to be built in the Picturesque manner until the artificially prolonged life of the system with which they were associated came to an end in the present century. The forms they took generally originated in

135 Homes for cottagers disguised as a massive villa displaying unrelated stylistic motifs, in the planned village of Edensor, Derbyshire, begun in 1839.

Opposite
XIII Carstone, set dry,
with brick dressings, at
Blackborough End in
Norfolk.

native styles, however feeble, distorted and confused the treatment. They might assume the comparatively sober shapes of cottages such as those in the village of Ridgmont on the Duke of Bedford's land or those built by Baron Dimsdale at Anstey in Hertfordshire, brick cottages grouped in twos or threes, gabled and with Gothic porches and Tudor chimneys. In a favourite mid-Victorian design, exemplified by some of the Audley End estate pairs of cottages, the bricks were red with ornaments of yellow brick, and bargeboarded gables dominated every elevation, those on the end walls decorated with rusticated Palladian niches. Later on, as at Elveden in Suffolk, the estate cottage might become almost indistinguishable from the final suburban manifestation of the Picturesque with sham half-timber in the front gable and rugged roughcast concealing the brick of the bay window. Alternatively, in the face of the break up of regional styles, the Picturesque impulse inspired nostalgic, self-conscious, vain attempts to reproduce them without exaggeration. The upper storeys of a group of estate cottages at Radwinter, Essex, designed by Eden Nesfield in 1877, are plastered and decorated with scattered pargework motifs of vaguely Baroque flavour which entirely fail to recapture the spirit of 17th-century pargetting, while a single-storeyed lodge at Moyns Park, timber-framed, plastered, neatly adorned with pargework bunches of grapes in panels about the window heads and with a pargework cock on the front of the two-storeyed porch, fails as signally to evoke the local vernacular. Looking at it, it is Warwickshire rather than Essex which first comes to mind.

The character of many estate cottages was a direct reflection of changes in society, of the ambiguous and unreal position of the country gentleman who acted the part of a feudal lord but whose estates were supported less and less by agricultural rents and more and more by investment and the proceeds of industry. But at the same time, owing to the accidents of history, numbers of cottages and farm buildings in areas untouched by industry went on testifying to the traditional skills of rural carpenters, bricklayers and masons. Those last survivals of the vernacular will appear in the course of the next chapter.

6
The Last of a Tradition

FOR THE BUILDINGS and way of life with which this book is concerned the most significant single event in the farming history of Queen Victoria's reign was the collapse of British agriculture in the 1870s. For this disaster slowed down the progress of industrialized farming, prolonged the life of the traditional homestead and halted the decay of the old village community until well into the present century. Of course the whole social fabric of rural life, depending as it did on inherited practices, was doomed from the moment the machines appeared on the scene and from the moment new communications by rail, road and canal were opened up. The break between old and new was an unavoidable consequence of changing attitudes to human endeavour and human labour; the race for material gain ineluctably destroyed the quality and harmony of ancient village self-sufficiency, individualism and pride in work.

In the decade preceding the collapse, the period known as the Golden Age, the advanced farm already foreshadowed the mechanized factory of today and when J. Wilson wrote his *British Farming* in 1862 he could refer to the farmstead as the farmer's manufactory with full confidence in the acceptability of the term. Enthusiasm for the poetry of the vernacular must not however be allowed to eclipse the glory of the farmer's achievement during those years of high prosperity. The population of the country had risen to more than twenty million by the 1860s, and all those mouths were fed without help or competition from overseas. Earlier methods of raising food for an expanding market were no longer relevant: reclamation could only go forward in the most limited way and enclosure was coming to an end. Between 1865 and 1875 the destruction of the remaining commons by enclosure was halted by the protest not of villagers but of the more articulate urban population, whose appreciation of rusticity, nurtured by the cult of the Picturesque, was heightened by the new and alarming conditions in the cities in which so huge a proportion of the English people were now living. The necessary increases in food production could only come from the more intensive cultivation of existing farmland and more intensive breeding of livestock. So the ideal Victorian farm was an industrialized version of its predecessors.

The almost obsessive interest in agriculture of the period was reflected in a mass of technical literature, particularly in articles published in the *Journal* of the Royal Agricultural Society, which had been founded in 1838 and

Opposite
XIV Brick- and stone-paved path leading directly to the door of a cottage at Welcombe, north Devon – the only part of the cottage garden where flowers are grown.

incorporated by Royal Charter in 1840 with the Queen as its patron. This literature discloses the same tendencies as the most up-to-date buildings of the time, for whereas earlier writings on husbandry are marked by a strong sense of regional diversity, in 19th-century publications discussion of local problems and local performances is submerged by the weight of information dealing with national agriculture. The farmer everywhere relied more and more on manufactured sources for feeding cattle, for fertilizers and for machinery and power. The work of the German chemist Liebig had revealed the intimate relation between the composition of the soil and the nutrition of plants and so had encouraged a keener and more widespread awareness of the connection between agriculture and science which resulted in the establishment of the experimental station at Rothamsted as early as 1843. The traditional farmer found himself relying on urban specialists: on the chemist who supplied substitutes for dung; on the many scientists in different fields who tested and defined the effects of food upon animals, verified the results of manuring on different soils and explained the scientific basis for the rotation of crops; and on the engineer who designed mass-produced implements in varieties never before seen – harrows suited to diverse operations, ploughs for every type of land which needed no sharpening, grubbers, cultivators and clod crushers and sheaf-delivering reapers like those shown in the revised edition of 1870 of Henry Stephens' *Book of the Farm*. One of the most profitable improvements on the farm was the development and installation of cylindrical drain pipes, mass-made by a machine patented by Thomas Scragg in 1845. Good drainage secured an earlier seedtime and an earlier harvest and increased the number of days on which it was possible to work the land. But the new system was not superior to the ancient East Anglian practice. There trenches of about 2 feet in depth were dug and then at the bottom of each of these another smaller channel was cut with a special wedge-shaped drainage tool. Boughs of thorn, heather or alder were tightly packed in this lower channel and the soil above them replaced. Water on the surface of the land percolated through the bush and found its way to the outlet of the drain in the side of the field ditch. Rider Haggard reported that this method was still used in Suffolk in 1902.

The threshing machine, an 18th-century invention which had been the focus of rural agitation and distress during the black period between the end of the Napoleonic wars and the accession of Queen Victoria, a time of poor harvests and dwindling rents, was now allied to a 19th-century power unit, the steam engine. The steam-driven triumph of urban industry seemed about to be repeated to the accompaniment of smoking chimneys in the harvest fields. One Yorkshire manufacturer turned spare-time farmer, a characteristic phenomenon of the age, described by Sir James Caird (who made an agricultural tour of the country in 1850–51), did realize this vision and with the aid of steam transformed his barn into a factory for grinding corn, crushing oil cake, pulping roots and converting all the farm produce into food for man and beast. Richard Jefferies too, in *Hodge and his Masters* (1880), draws a portrait from life of a progressive Wiltshire farmer whose outlook and methods thoroughly anticipate those of the typical farmer of the 1980s. For him farming was 'emphatically "business" the same as iron,

Opposite
136 Village pump,
Pembridge, Herefordshire
(see p. 195).

coal or cotton'. The beat of the engines never seemed to cease on his land; all the hedges had been grubbed up and the whole of his arable had been thrown into one vast field and levelled with the theodolite. The land had been drained at enormous cost and was irrigated by a centrifugal pump. Tons of artificial manure were brought by canal to the farm. Chaff cutters, root pulpers and winnowing machines were all driven by steam and a light railway transported men and materials from one part of the farm to another. Just as on the late 20th century farm, the accounts and administrative work were dealt with in a specially built office equipped with the apparatus of the most modern business techniques.

But very few farmers could afford such machine-aided efficiency; and as Richard Jefferies' 'Man of Progress' remarked, it was not easy to introduce scientific farming into England in the face of tradition and custom. In any case that man came to grief in the years of the depression – as did a farmer at Littlebury, Essex, and others who had invested extensively in the new machines. Sales catalogues of the last quarter of the 19th century show that mechanization on farms was largely confined to various drilling and reaping machines, turnip cutters, oil cake mills, bean crushers and root pulpers. And although some farmers might dream of self-moving ploughs, the chief use they found for steam power was in the form of a mobile engine by means of which corn was threshed in the fields instead of in the barn. The sight of corn being threshed in the harvest field was still common for some years after the Second World War.

But the steam engine did not revolutionize farmstead planning even if the ways in which it was used by a few of the wealthiest and most mechanically minded farmers did change the functions of the barn. It was a long time before the machine was generally accepted. In southern England the flail was almost universally used for threshing, partly to ensure that labourers should be supplied with winter work. In the north the horse-driven gin gang continued in use at least until the 1930s. Mr Ridley of Chollerton readily recalled in conversation in 1953 the gin gangs in operation in his corner of Northumberland some twenty years earlier and spoke of the amazing agility and docility of the horses. Horses were indeed much more widely used than steam to drive machines right up to the early decades of the present century, and the Suffolk Punch was recognized as the finest draught horse. This splendid creature, called Punch because his smooth legs are rather short and his body is barrel shaped, like those of Mr Punch, was – in common with other Shire horses such as the 'Large Black Old English Cart Horse' and the Cleveland Bay – descended from animals originally bred to bear the weight of armoured men on the battlefield. Enclosure and the consequent replacement of the ox by the horse were favourable to the heavy breeds and the second half of the 18th century was a formative period. But the full development of the draught horse, especially the Suffolk Punch, belongs to the Victorian era when Thomas Crisp of Butley Abbey perfected the chestnut coach horse bred by his ancestor and namesake at Ufford towards the end of the previous century.

At the time of the depression, despite some scientific innovations, nothing had yet disturbed the intimacy of the relationship between the farmer and the animals on whom he was dependent for his livelihood.

When Victorian farms were sold up, as they were in great numbers at that time, the animals were usually listed by name. In 1884 the working horses on Justice's Farm, at Finchingfield in Essex, were Gilbert, Ball, Charlie, Captain, Prince, Boxer and Depper; Mr Buller's stables at nearby Newport housed Polley, Smiler, Short, Moco, Boxer, William and Peg. Cows were not then merely 'livestock', but were still, as they always had been, individual creatures who answered to their names, typical of which and tending to recur on widely separated farms were Cherry, Snowflake, Cowslip and Judy, Tulip, Rose, Brindle, Polly and Spotty. Bulls were often called Rufus and Orion.

Just as farming methods based on traditional wisdom handed down from generation to generation and on the farmer's personal experience, observation and detailed knowledge of the subtle differences between field and field were beginning to be supplanted, theoretically if only occasionally in fact, by the precepts of agricultural science, expert soil analysis and the application of text-book rules, so the buildings demanded by this more exacting farming were also beginning to be supplied by specialists from the city and the village craftsman's skill was becoming irrelevant. Although in his *Farm Homesteads of England* (1863) J. Denton conceded that 'local materials should not hastily be set aside', he hastened to point out that imported timber, standardized bricks and Welsh slates transported by rail were cheaper than those materials; and many newly invented substances were appearing on the farm.

Concrete was used as the foundation for all good farm buildings, and concrete blocks were being made as early as 1860. An article in the *Journal of the Royal Agricultural Society* in 1874 actually proposed concrete as a suitable building material for cottages as well as farm buildings. The first concrete farm building was a fattening shed with a tiled roof erected in about 1870 at Faringdon in Berkshire by Robert Campbell. A farmstead on the Cambridgeshire-Essex borders near Duxford, a rectangular yard with livestock buildings and cartsheds of traditional plan, was constructed almost entirely of concrete about twenty years later and still stands as sullenly and uncooperatively in the landscape as when it made its first appearance. Factory-made asphalt was used for flooring; creosote had been applied to timber as a preservative by 1840; and corrugated iron sheeting, appreciated for its cheapness and lightness, appeared on roofs and was also used for walls. Sometimes a cottage even might be fashioned of this material, and although totally alien to any landscape, the pictorial effect, unlike that of concrete, could be amusing and folly-like. The little house on a smallholding at Bawdsey, Suffolk, one of many created to help rural XI labourers during the depression, artlessly assumes the traditional design of a central block with cross-wings, the corrugated iron walls painted viridian, the corrugated iron roof and lean-to porch vermilion, the incredible colours and wavy surfaces vibrating to the harmonies of the shingle beach and the marshes between which it stands.

Prefabricated parts, mostly of cast iron, came from the factory to modernize barn, stable and byre. The 1884 catalogue of the hardware merchants Pfeil, Stedall & Sons of Bloomsbury, London, shows illustrations of cast-iron stall divisions, mangers and pig troughs, bases for stall posts, cow ties, ventilation sashes for stables, rails and rollers for sliding doors, farmyard gates, stable gutters of ornamental design and portable farmyard boilers. The farmer was already able to buy the commonest and simplest 137 structure on the farm, the Dutch barn, ready made and consisting of steel members and corrugated iron sheeting. All he had to do was to prepare the concrete foundation and a gang of workmen sent by the manufacturer would then erect the industrially produced barn. Henry Stephens noted that such barns were very plentiful and they were to be seen on farms in every part of the country earlier in the present century.

The basic farm buildings changed little in principle during Victoria's reign, though published plans included prophetic designs heralding the conditions of the modern factory farm. Farmyard fowls were by and large still allowed to scrap round the kitchen door and roost in the barn and hay loft; but in an article written in 1866 J. A. Clarke describes a building like a vast greenhouse, more than 300 feet long, for the production of eggs and table poultry by mechanically precise means.

Clarke's article was published in the *Journal of the Royal Agricultural Society* and the impression made by leafing through this periodical is that the industrial and scientific approach to farming had left little room for traditional methods and that by the end of the last century the farmer was already the urbanized and unrecognizable John Bull he has since become. Yet though the expansion of agriculture was one of the most notable manifestations of the age, when Caird went on his tour of the country he observed that the majority of farmers had adapted existing vernacular buildings to more productive methods, that most of them set as much store by intuition and experience as by the new scientific and mechanical procedures, and that a desk in the parlour and one or two documents stuffed behind the clock on the kitchen mantelshelf were the average farmer's nearest approach to an office.

It is clear from the testimony of writers such as George Borrow, Thomas Hardy and Flora Thompson that although the village was no longer a self-contained community, though the recently introduced village shop was stocked with goods from the cities and from overseas, and although the age of the local craftsman was passing, the immemorial customs of rural life had not come to an end. The calamity which from about 1875 onwards followed on the repeal of the Corn Laws, a sequence of unkind seasons and the importation (by means of new steamers and new railway systems) of frozen meat from Australia, New Zealand and South America and above all of cheap grain from the limitless cornfields of America, halted the progress of industrialized farming. 'Prolonged depression', writes Lord Ernle, 'checked costly improvements. Drainage was practically discontinued. Both owners and occupiers were engaged in the task of making both ends meet on vanishing incomes. Land deteriorated in condition; less labour was employed; less stock was kept; bills for cake and fertilizers were reduced.'

The sufferings occasioned by these conditions have been often and eloquently portrayed. They were as acute in counties like Essex where mixed farming was still practised, where many flocks of sheep still grazed in the pastures and where weaving was still carried on in some of the cottages, as in Suffolk which had become predominantly arable. Many farmers,

137 Prefabricated Dutch barn, Shipton Hill, Dorset.

unable to stock their farms, abandoned them; and the plight of the agricultural labourer, especially in the open villages where there was no resident squire to regulate migration and where tradesmen from the expanding towns were buying up derelict cottages and letting them to farmhands just as they stood, was often appalling. Contemporary descriptions show scene after scene of misery – a father, mother and six children crowded together in one bedroom at Burwell, Cambridgeshire in 1874; a labourer at Barrow, Suffolk, whose bedroom was so tiny, only 7 feet 6 inches by 6 feet 9 inches, that he could not shift his poor bed away from the rain dripping through a hole in the roof. Richard Heath, author of *The English Peasantry* (1874), had been into a cottage at Rotherfield in Sussex where ten hungry children and their mother huddled in two bedrooms, one of which contained nothing but a makeshift bed on the floor.

Oppression and near starvation led to union activity and the organization under Joseph Arch of the Warwickshire Agricultural Labourers' Union. Unrest, emigration and a drift to the towns threatened the continuity of rural life: as Jefferies remarked, there was 'a general feeling in the villages and agricultural districts that the landed estates around them are no longer stable and enduring. A feeling of uncertainty is abroad, and no-one is surprised to hear that some place, or person, is going.' The rumblings of catastrophic upheaval mutter in the background of the whole agricultural scene. Yet the time when farming ceased to be a way of life and became one industry among many still lay in the future.

Because the increase in food production came chiefly from the more intensive exploitation of existing steadings, only a small number of new farmhouses were built during the Victorian period, some to serve land won from the last wildernesses, others to replace village homesteads by farmhouses in the enclosed fields. As for cottages, landowners continued to build homes for the men working on their farms. The new farmhouses and cottages usually displayed some symptoms of a disintegrating tradition: it was only in areas remote from large towns and not easily reached by the new forms of transport that they remained the unselfconscious creations of local craftsmen. A farmhouse designed by Eden Nesfield near Crewe Green, Cheshire perfectly exemplifies a late phase of the Picturesque style at its most indeterminate, for it combines tile-hanging in the style of Kent or Sussex with half-timber work reminiscent of East Anglia. Another farmhouse in the same district, Leighton Hall Farm, many-gabled and with tall chimneys adorned with classical niches, is constructed of locally made bricks of mottled brown and pink colour though the roof is of Welsh slate and the elevations and general eclectic aspect are almost identical with those of a farmhouse near Trumpington in distant Cambridgeshire.

The interiors of these farmhouses included more rooms than either the traditional or the Georgian farmhouse: in addition to a large kitchen and a dairy with a scalding room leading from it there were store rooms, a pump room, a parlour, a dining room and the modish 'morning room'. This is just the kind of farmhouse which Jefferies visited in Wiltshire in the 1870s. He describes it as more of a large villa-like mansion than a farm. The parlour was filled with rosewood and ormolu, ottomans and 'occasional' tables and furnished with 'semi-ecclesiastical' grate fittings. Glass glittered everywhere: there were mirrors over the mantelpieces and mirrors let into panels and prisms of glass dangled from the candlesticks. The dining room was resplendent with an array of electroplate and round the table stood a set of straight-backed oak chairs of medieval flavour.

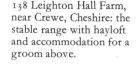

138 Leighton Hall Farm, near Crewe, Cheshire: the stable range with hayloft and accommodation for a groom above.

None of the more dramatic innovations recommended in the technical journals are encountered in the Leighton Hall farm buildings except that the open yards are rather larger than those of earlier steadings, the barn is small and the cowhouse and stable are floored with concrete and well drained. They are of brick and in the style of the previous century with haylofts pierced by roundels and with ventilation holes making geometric patterns in the fabric. The doors are all painted a traditional deep blood red.

Another Cheshire farmhouse, at Stretton, realizes a prim, compressed design from C. A. Audsley's *Cottage, Lodge and Villa Architecture* in which the plans and elevations show earnest, somewhat forbidding Victorian versions of the Picturesque Gothic, Elizabethan, Italian and 'Old Scotch' styles. The façade, behind the cast-iron gate and whitewashed concrete piers of a suburban villa, is of Tudor derivation and the sharply pointed, narrow gables and tall chimneys primly condense and parody the image of Manor Farm, Toseland. Nonetheless its plum-coloured tiles and dark bricks, sandstone lintels and sandstone gable outlines all belong to the region.

Brook Farm, at King's Pyon in Herefordshire, offers a greater affront to local tradition: not only does the classical temple portico show no evidence of the rural craftsman's personal interpretation of the pattern-book design, but the whole brick façade has been limewashed to imitate stucco, that substitute material of which John Nash was the master and which, essentially theatrical and *trompe l'œil*, was a prime destroyer of the vernacular. Blank sash windows of commercially produced sheet glass stare across standardized cast-iron railings topped by gilded ornaments such as were still being advertised by O'Brien, Thomas and Company of London at the end of the 19th century. Fortunately a sense of place and of reality is restored by a pretty dovecote, brick nogged and of late, probably 18th-century date, but still expressive of the black-and-white tradition of Herefordshire.

139 Brook Farm, King's Pyon, Herefordshire.

71

139

A few instances of 19th-century cottages in closed villages and on the farms of great estates have already been seen. Some landlords converted farmhouses, which had been left empty by the amalgamation of two or more farms, into cottages for labourers, as they had done earlier. The Earl of Stradbroke, for example, turned an old farmhouse at Sotherton in Suffolk into three dwellings, each consisting of a sizeable living room, washhouse, good pantry and two bedrooms, and either a second pantry, a cellar or an attic. A considerable number of new estate cottages built during the second half of the Victorian period had three bedrooms. The forms they took were generally Picturesque and disruptive of local tradition. Cottages built for farmhands in the 1870s at Sudbury, Derbyshire – for Lord Vernon to the design of an architect from Derby – could scarcely be more unlike the traditional cottage of that region. Paired and taking the form of a cluster of steeply gabled projections, from the middle of which rises a tight, rectangular mass of ornate chimneys, their light brick walls are richly patterned with deep red headers, bands, and arch and gable shapes. Narrow lancets light the smaller of the three bedrooms, while the main windows are of Tudor form. Side porches like those of a church, with ogee entrances and precipitous roofs, lead solemnly into a high-ceilinged living room with a capacious scullery and pantry behind it and a fuel store and pigsty close to the back door.

Pallid machine-pressed bricks were used for a terrace of six cottages at Southwell, Nottinghamshire. The pantiles of the roofs were probably made in the county, but Welsh slate protects the latticed porches and the heavily bargeboarded and half-timbered attic dormers. Another row of six
140 dwellings at Warter, Yorkshire, reveals even less of its geographical situation. Of whitewashed brick, thickly thatched and with counterfeit half-timber in the dormer gables and above the doors of the thatched and latticed porches, the home counties might well have given them birth. The accommodation provided by such cottages was, however, much better than that of the cramped and insanitary hovels of the open villages. The front doors at Southwell opened directly into the parlour, but there was a passage leading to the stairs at Warter. On the ground floor there were two rooms, a scullery and an ample larder. The attics at Southwell seem never to have been used as bedrooms, however large the family, but for storage.

140 *Below* Cottage row, Warter, Yorkshire.

141 *Below right* Rat-trap bond brickwork at Henlow, Bedfordshire.

Some new cottages, just as unrelated to their settings, were erected in open villages, generally for urban landlords. In the Cheviots near Kirknewton a row of six such dwellings unite in one brick frontage, the eaves of the slate roofs broken by six dormers, a feature as unlikely in this region as the materials, to house the workers on a farm – a fragment of back-street city housing misjoined to that majestic and desolate landscape of huge rounded russet hills and stone walls. And the commonest form taken by the speculative builder's cottage was of urban origin, two-storeyed, four-roomed, of brick and paired or part of a terrace, like those at Henlow, Bedfordshire, where in some of the little dwellings, to save cost, 141 the bricks are laid on edge in the style known as 'rat-trap bond'.

While mass-produced and standardized materials were finding their way into most country districts, Welsh slate even making a dramatic appearance on the gable end of a timber-framed cottage at Ivinghoe, Buckinghamshire,

142 Farm labourers' cottages near Kirknewton, Northumberland.

in the form of fishscale cladding of mechanical uniformity, the vernacular tradition was still very much alive in the more inaccessible areas. Villages described by Hardy were nearly as self-sufficient as they had been two centuries earlier: the prominent figures in the community, apart from the squire and the farmers with their carters, shepherd and labourers, were still the blacksmith, the mason, the thatcher, the miller and the baker. William Crossing, the author of *A Hundred Years on Dartmoor*, written at the end of the last century, had recently seen labourers living under the same roof as their cattle on food produced on their own patches of rough land – barley bread, potatoes, leeks, onions and bacon. Their cottages were of granite crudely thatched.

In parts of East Anglia local craftsmen continued to show fresh vigorous invention in the use of flints. In Norfolk, many later farm buildings are simply and straightforwardly constructed of tweedy-textured flint roofed with pantiles. Similar flints, alternately chalk-coated and displaying their gleaming hearts, are held on the walls of a cottage at Hingham in a light red network of brick diamonds and hexagons; the builder of a cottage at East

144 Raynham chose the biggest and most irregular flints he could find for a tiny symmetrical front with twin pert miniature bay windows, and its dynamic rugosity surpasses the liveliest of earlier achievements in this medium. A row of labourers' cottages at Saffron Walden in Essex, constructed of equally rough but smaller stones, glitters with the same bursting vitality, only just restrained here by bold bands of red brick. Kidney cobbles were never made into walls of more pleasingly homespun character than those of two small cottages at Uggeshall, Suffolk.

143 *Below* Flint galleted with clinkers at Stoke Ferry, Norfolk.

144 *Below right* Flint and brick at East Raynham, Norfolk.

145 *Above* Clunch and brick at Burnham Overy, Norfolk.

146 *Right* Kidney cobbles, pantiles and clematis, Uggeshall, Suffolk.

Again in Norfolk, dusky red local brick and alternating chalky white flints speckle the glinting façade of a very modest farmhouse at Great Massingham, while a pair of cottages at Stoke Ferry of near suburban form 143 is transfigured by the adventurous treatment of the walls: they are fashioned of irregular flints interspersed here and there with red brick and galletted with tiny black clinkers. At Burnham Overy a ground floor of 145 strong red brick is unexpectedly topped by a first floor of staring white clunch. That strange material peculiar to Norfolk, carstone, which had XIII already made a tentative appearance in local buildings, came into its own at 132 the very time when vernacular styles and crafts were in jeopardy. Small thin slabs of the sandy yellow and dark brown substance were used dry and with quoins and window frames of pale ochre brick to make a forceful impact at Blackborough End in two joined cottages of otherwise undistinguished and untraditional design.

Farther afield, cottages of the same plan as those at Henlow, a much 141 pared down and degenerate version of the Georgian terrace house, might, as at Bonsall in Derbyshire, be both rooted and animated by the use of local stone. Two pygmy cottages built at Green How, Yorkshire, in 1854, later made into one, given the grand name of Groom House and inhabited by a shepherd, top a bleak hill, a trenchant emanation of it with their walls of dark sandstone and heavy stone slates.

New farmhouses in the north might occasionally take the form of a freestanding rectangle lit by sash windows of unrelieved sheet glass, but more often the style of the native long-house was retained and the materials

189

147 The long-house tradition persists in this farmhouse at Dufton, Westmorland, but there is no communication between house and farm buildings. The group is known as a 'laithe house' ('laithe' means a combined barn and byre) because it adjoins a barn and byre.

were those of ancient usage. A wonderfully harmonious example, the farmstead stretched against the high fells at Dufton, Westmorland, was described at the beginning of this book in relation to the primeval custom which it continues (p. 16). And when at Newlands Hall Farm, Frosterley, Co. Durham, a new house was built in the late 19th century it continued the line of the earlier long-house (see the frontispiece, p. 2).

Life inside more distant farmhouses such as this sometimes continued with very little change into the present century. At Hodge Hill Farm, Cartmel Fell, Lancashire, the home in the early 1950s of a lady farmer as forceful as Hardy's Bathsheba Everdene, if a good deal older, the furniture in the cavernous living room or house-place included, apart from fine examples of the screen-cupboards of the region, a long oak table with a bench on one side of it, a waxed chest with a carved back that turned it into a settle, an eight-day clock ticking loudly in a tall case and a big dresser on which pewter plates shone amid a mixed collection of mugs and beer jugs. Bread was still baked in the oven beside the generous hearth, and this small farm was one of the very few where at that time butter and cheese were still made in the dairy. The scene was little different from the interior of Hall Farm so vividly evoked a hundred years earlier by George Eliot in *Adam Bede*, with its bright cool dairy and its shining house-place with scrubbed floor, high mantelshelf set with brass candlesticks, brilliantly polished clock case and its oak table, usually turned up like a screen. And that room would have looked much the same a century earlier still. Mrs Gaskell's description of the parlour and house-place at Hope Farm in *Cousin Phillis* breathes a most comforting sense of continuity and tradition, and unforgettably conjures up the atmosphere of a remote country interior, not only of the time at which she was writing (1863), but such as could still be experienced by anyone old enough to appreciate it almost a hundred years later:

> The parlour was a large room with two casemented windows on the other side of the broad flagged passage leading from the rector-door to the wide staircase, with its shallow, polished oaken steps, on which no carpet was ever laid. The parlour floor was covered in the middle by a home-made carpetting of needlework and list. One or two quaint family pictures of the Holman family hung round the walls; the fire-grate and irons were much ornamented with brass; and on a table against the wall between the windows, a great beau-pot of flowers was placed upon the folio volumes of Matthew Henry's Bible. . . . The large house-place, living-room, dining-room, whichever you might like to call it, was twice as comfortable and cheerful. There was a rug in front of the great large fire-place, and an oven by the grate, and a crook with the kettle hanging from it, over the bright wood-fire; everything that ought to be black and polished in that room was black and polished; and the flags, and window-curtains and such things as were to be white and clean, were just spotless in their purity. Opposite to the fire-place, extending the whole length of the room, was an oaken shovel-board, with the right incline for a skilful player to send the weights into the prescribed place. There were baskets of white work about, and a small shelf of books hung against the wall, books used for reading, and not for propping up a beau-pot of flowers.

The prosperous mid-Victorian years of high farming naturally brought changes to some farmhouse interiors, especially if the farm lay within reach of a sizeable town, and there were numbers of rooms which were not unlike those which so outraged Jefferies. Because after a short period of affluence, when they had accumulated more possessions than had ever been seen in modest rural dwellings, numbers of farmers were forced to sell up during the depression to discharge their debts, auctioneers have sometimes preserved minutely detailed catalogues of the contents of farmhouses and farm buildings. Remarkably complete records for north-west Essex exist for the whole of Victoria's reign and they reflect most of the fashionable additions to the home.

Old farmhouses were altered and enlarged to create the rooms which were considered essential in newly built homesteads such as the one near Crewe. Gifford's Farm, Little Sampford, where the house was of modest size, consisted in 1845 of the 'keeping room' (or living room), the parlour, a pantry, washhouse and dairy on the ground floor, a 'little chamber', servant's chamber, 'middle room', bedroom and linen cupboard on the first floor, and above that an attic and a man servant's room. The word 'chamber' was used less and less frequently during the second half of the century and the term 'bedroom' became general. Sometimes the bedrooms in larger houses might be given such pretentious names as the Red Room, the Blue Room or the Grey Room. The parlour kept its name, though in sale catalogues of the 1880s it is called the 'Drawing Room' and on one occasion it becomes the 'Front Room', a term later associated with the best room in little town houses. At the end of the 19th century the breakfast room, the dining room, the drawing room and the morning room were found in many farmhouses; the 'keeping room' had become the 'sitting room'. There might also be a 'gun room'.

During the years of prosperity farmers and their wives filled these rooms with new furniture and fashionable ornaments, though older tables and Windsor and ladderback chairs seem to have been kept and at New House Farm, Wimbish there was still an oak hutch of 17th-century date in 1884. The keeping room at Hole Farm, Little Sampford, when the contents and farming stock were sold on 20 November 1844, was furnished with a large oval dining table, a small deal table, a flap table of the kind which appeared in the early 18th century, an eight-day clock, five elbow chairs and six 'flat-seat' chairs, and a 'beaufet' (a new name for the sideboard, a backless version of the dresser), together with a set of fire irons and a fender, a baking pan, a dripping pan and a cleaver, a brass ladle, a round copper boiler and a chimney crane and hooks. There were two meat safes in the pantry and a few tubs, but carpenter's tools were also kept there; indeed it seems to have served as a lumber room, for it contained a fire screen, a cob iron, a brass boiler, a cupboard and 'sundries'. In the parlour stood another dining table and an oval table and fourteen chairs, among which six were mahogany with fashionable horsehair seats. There was in addition a painted 'beaufet' with nine wine and beer glasses standing on it as well as a tea tray and tea service. Various ornaments and a pair of brass candlesticks garnished the mantelshelf and six paintings adorned the walls. The three bedrooms, still called 'chambers', all contained wooden bedsteads, two of which were four-posters. In one of them was a 'wardrobe' – a word which was beginning to replace the 'hanging-press' or 'press-cupboard' of earlier inventories.

When we turn to the kitchen, dairy and farmyard, where the work of Hole Farm was done, the equipment differs little from that of earlier centuries. It is true that the iron boiler in the kitchen would formerly have been of copper or brass and the table might not have been of deal, but the familiar cob irons, gridiron, roaster, hob iron, peel and oven fork, skillet and stand, copper and brass pots, pot hangers, brewing copper and kneading trough were all present among the bowls, pitchers, bottles and cream pots. In the dairy stood a barrel churn, a milk stand and milk pail, four milk pans, a pair of butter scales, two cream pots, several pork pots, a pork tub and a quantity of pork. Down in the cellar were stored five hogshead (54-gallon) casks, six half-hogshead casks, an 18-gallon cask, ale stalls (to save bending low over tubs and casks), a 'runnel' (funnel of wood) and a tap 'ooze' (hose), five wort tubs and a jet, a mash tub and four one-gallon stone bottles. The tap was used to draw off the wort (the liquid which had percolated through the mash of malt in the first stage of beer-making) from the mash tub, so that the hops could be boiled in it. The large number of implements at Hole Farm included nothing more up to date than an iron breast plough for three horses and four iron harrows. A wooden plough was still in use. Among the livestock were two carthorses, Short and Prince, as well as a pony, a herd of shorthorn cows and yard fowls.

A bankrupt tenant farmer of Hobs Aerie, Arkesden, whose possessions were all sold on 28 February 1887, had lived more grandly in a house with more rooms. On the ground floor were the kitchen, a store room, the brewhouse and dairy, the 'right hand room', the housemaid's closet, the breakfast room, dining room, drawing room and hall, while upstairs there were two main bedrooms, one with a dressing room adjoining it, a back bedroom and a servant's room. The brewhouse contained all the traditional utensils and gadgets, including the 'underback' (the broad, low tub into which the wort was put when drawn off from the mash tub before being transferred to the copper) and a set of steelyards, a form of scale in which a counterpoise was moved along a graduated beam. One new piece of equipment was kept in the brewhouse, Bradford's Patent Washing Machine.

The Arkesden house was crammed with objects, among which some were mass-produced and of recent origin. In the kitchen, where the floor was covered with 'coco' matting, there was a paraffin stove together with four oil lamps; against the wall stood a new article of furniture known as the 'Davenport', a form of writing table. A new green and white dinner service in 74 pieces and a 'Chinese' tea set in 29 pieces were kept in the store room. There was a great deal of mahogany and horsehair furniture in the principal rooms draped with antimacassars and including one of those horsehair couches with a roll at one end, not quite high enough to permit sitting up in comfort, but which nevertheless made all thought of going to sleep on it out of the question. There was an 'old oak table' in the breakfast room and the dining-room chairs had leather seats. In this room there was also a tripod table, and paired vases and ornaments adorned the mantelshelf. Brussels carpets and Brussels rugs enriched the floors. Among the pictures were two watercolour landscapes, a set of 'Fox-Hunting' prints, a framed engraving, an oil painting and a map of Essex. In the breakfast room there were ninety-four bound volumes of popular periodicals. An umbrella stand and a stuffed magpie and stuffed gull under glass domes were conspicuous objects in the hall, where the boards were covered with 'floor cloth and coco mats'. On the upstairs landing was a large flower stand displaying potted plants.

While in the living rooms the curtains were of 'moreen', a new heavy material of mixed wool and cotton, in the bedrooms they were of muslin or green damask. The bedsteads, except for one of mahogany in the back bedroom (so it was little esteemed), were no longer of wood but of fashionable cast iron. Marble-topped washstands figured prominently, furnished with sets of green and white jugs, basins and soap dishes. The dressing room contained not only a washstand with a 'japanned' toilet set (black-stained, in imitation of lacquer) and a mahogany towel rail, but a bath standing on a piece of felt carpet and a mahogany night commode. The servant's room was provided with a painted washstand and another, corner, washstand, a japanned French bed with a flock mattress, a 'Queen Ann' glass and a toilet table with a framed mahogany mirror. A crib and bedding for it were kept in this room together with five bushels of potatoes and, most unexpectedly, a double-barrelled 12-bore breech loader.

The Siggs family of New House Farm, Wimbish, had furnished their house in similar style. Here the davenport was more suitably installed in the drawing room, where there was also a walnut loo table and where a glass in a fine gilt frame hung above the fireplace. The carpets, as they seem to have been in many farmhouses of that time, were either Brussels or

Kidderminster, and one of them had a flowered border. The hall was decorated with stuffed squirrels and stuffed jays in cases and with antique pistols; it was lit by large bronze candlesticks, a wall barometer hung near the door, and beside it stood an eight-day clock in a wainscot case. Mahogany and horsehair furnished the dining room together with a dwarf armchair and an easy chair, both covered in oiled American cloth. On a rosewood writing table inlaid with brass stood a rosewood workbox and a case of stuffed hummingbirds. On the walls hung seven coloured prints of hunting scenes in maple frames and two needlework pictures. The upstairs landing was furnished, as at Arkesden, with a flower stand and also with a stool, three shells and a doll's bedstead. There were four bedrooms with either mahogany or cast-iron beds. In the 'second bedroom' there was another stuffed bird, a kingfisher, under a glass dome, an engraving of Lord Nelson in a gilt frame hung on the wall, and two bronzed plaster figures and three 'figured' chimney ornaments graced the mantelpiece. There were two dressing glasses in mahogany frames in this room and two chests of drawers, as well as a dressing table and a painted washstand and two mahogany bonnet stands. In the same room also stood a white foot bath, a tin water can and a hip bath. Besides dinner, dessert and tea services, some of which were 'green and white' like those at Arkesden, and a quantity of glass, the Siggses possessed some Spode and Lowestoft bowls, basins, cups, plates and a teapot. The kitchen, brewhouse and dairy remained traditional, displaying copper warming pans, gridirons, roasting jacks, copper pots, brass preserving pans, wort and mash tubs, runnel and jet, cheese presses and moulds, skimmers and strainers, churn and keeler (cooler), though there was one novelty – Ransome's Patent Mangle, which was of cast iron with wooden rollers.

The tenant of Freeman's Farm in the same parish, who only a year earlier, in 1883, had to sell all his implements, stock and household goods 'under a Distress for Rent', furnished the interior of his 17th-century timber-framed house in much the same way again – although it was considerably smaller with only a 'sitting room', kitchen and dairy on the ground floor and three bedrooms and a lumber room above. He had an American clock in a mahogany frame on the kitchen wall and the same room was furnished with four old Windsor chairs and a painted dresser. An old trestle table of the type listed in early inventories as a 'planke table' stood in the dairy. In the sitting room, as well as the usual mahogany-framed horsehair chairs, a mahogany loo table and a gate-legged table there was a piece of furniture which was rapidly becoming a status symbol, the upright piano – here a 'six and a half cottage piano' by 'T. Smith'.

Another piece of furniture which was occasionally seen now in the farmhouse was the mahogany or rosewood 'cheffonier' (akin to the sideboard); and the tiered mahogany 'what-not' (a set of small shelves for the display of knick-knacks) and the ottoman were popular household gods. Besides oil paintings and prints the farmhouse pictures now included oleographs. Oil lamps are listed in most sale catalogues but many rooms were candle-lit. Hangings were often of the machine-printed chintz and cretonne which had replaced the hand-blocked cottons of the 18th century. In some farmhouses there was no sign of a book other than the Family

Bible, though the Reynoldses of Gifford's Farm, Little Sampford, had a shelf in the keeping room on which were two Bibles, 'sundry books' and six volumes of *Doddridge's Family Expositor*. Mr Osborn of Quendon owned Whitfield's sermons and twelve other books; and Captain R. Bird Thompson, who was farming at Little Walden Hall until 1885, when he had to sell up and leave the neighbourhood, owned a collection of books which were characteristic of the taste of the period. They were *Dwight's Theology* in five volumes, Horseley's *Book of Psalms* and *Biblical Fragments*, *Macknight on the Epistles* and Butterworth's *Concordance*, the works of Cowper and Cowley, *The British Essayist* in six volumes, Bingley's *Animal Biography*, Pinnock's *Guide to Knowledge* and ten years of *The Field*. Captain Bird Thompson also owned a magic lantern and twelve slides and an egg cabinet fitted with drawers and an 'excellent collection of birds' eggs'.

With all their fashionable furnishings and furniture, much of which, if we are to judge from survivals, was made by country joiners as inventive as their predecessors, it seems that old traditions were still upheld on these Essex farms. Conditions remained almost static from the time when the contents were listed until after the Second World War, when, from the 1950s onwards, the industrialized farm visualized by the Victorians did not only rapidly become fact but took forms beyond the dreams of even Jefferies' progressive Cecil. It was not very common before this period of intensive factory farming had got under way to come across an interior like that of Hodge Hill Farm where no piece of furniture was of later date than 1800, but it was extremely common to find farm kitchens much like those of Hole Farm and New House Farm – though both the dairy and brew-house were seldom used and though 'convenience' foods and sliced bread were often enough put on the farmhouse table. In the fields the implements which had been introduced in the 19th century were still widely used. A two-horse mowing machine of wood and iron such as was produced by the Yorkshire firm of A.C. Bamlett, Ltd, was at work in the fields of Little Langdale, Westmorland, just as it had been a hundred years earlier, soon after this type of machine was singled out by the Yorkshire Agricultural Society for its steady motion and absence of friction.

The outshot back kitchen at Hillside Farm, Hapton, Norfolk, seen a few years after the end of the Second World War, with its big bread oven, copper, oil lamps still in use, pot boiling on an open fire and coco matting on the uneven flagged and tiled floor, showed few signs of change though electricity had been installed a month or two earlier and Lucy the servant was using an electric iron. In a similar kitchen at Pembridge, Herefordshire, a kitchen range filled the fireplace opening and á stone copper against the wall at right angles to the range (with a zinc bucket and an oil cooking stove standing on it) conveniently adjoined the sink. Such sinks, of stone, shallow and with a gentle slope, sometimes called 'slop-stones', had been a normal feature of manor houses since the 16th century but had only been common in small farmhouses from about 1750. The one at Pembridge was connected by a lead pipe to a runlet outside, but there was no tap in the house. Water had to be fetched, as it still was in many rural districts, from a communal pump. At Frog's Hall, Biddenden, the kitchen hearth of which has already appeared in these pages, the farmhouse had its own pump set

148

150

136
119

148 *Above left* The kitchen, Hillside Farm, Hapton, Norfolk.

149 *Above* The pantry, Harthill Hall Farm, Alport, Derbyshire. The partly timber-framed wall separates it from the dairy.

150 *Left* Cottage kitchen, Pembridge, Herefordshire.

beside a splendid example of the traditional sink, constructed of the same brick as the floor. Next to the sink stood a cast-iron and wooden mangle just like the one used at New House Farm, Wimbish, some seventy years earlier. At Mr and Mrs Abbott's in Matterdale, Cumberland, the sink had been fitted into a corner of the house-place (as it continued to be called in the north): it was still shallow but was of dark brown glazed earthenware of Victorian manufacture, surrounded by pretty Victorian transfer-printed tiles. Water had only been brought to the little farmstead two years before the time of our visit.

Pantries had for the most part not then been modernized and re-frigerators were never seen on small farms. The pantry at Harthill Hall Farm, at Alport in Derbyshire, lit by a deeply embrasured window, with one stone and several wooden shelves set against the cool, whitewashed walls to hold finely glazed earthen pots and bowls of local workmanship and a number of standardized pudding basins, is typical of many except for the meagre store of provisions it contains. Mr Twyford was an elderly bachelor farmer and lived alone in the old house that was formerly the home of the aristocratic Derbyshire Cockayne family.

The cottage interiors of the older generation of farmworkers in the 1950s had remained extraordinarily like those so movingly because so faithfully described by Flora Thompson in the opening chapters of *Lark Rise*. They combined a sense of old tradition with collections of objects which might include both earlier and Victorian pieces of furniture and ornaments, but little of 20th-century date except family photographs – of which there were generally a great number – and photographs of the Royal Family.

Mr Moseley, a bachelor cottager of Lightmoor, Shropshire, cooked on an open fire before which stood a bright steel trivet, steel tongs, poker and shovel and handsome steel firedogs joined by bars, all of 18th-century date. But the cast-iron kitchen range was an almost universal feature of unaltered cottages, generally with a central open fire with an oven on one side of it and perhaps a small boiler on the other. The original wide fireplace of old cottages was usually filled in, as could be seen in a cottage at Nunney, Somerset; but at old Mrs Bowditch's in Crewkerne the 'kitchener' was set right at the back of the original opening, still leaving an inglenook. In front of the central grate there was often a profusely decorated cast-iron three-sided movable object jutting out almost to the fender. There was one in Mrs Holman's cottage at Crewkerne and another in young Mrs Bowditch's. They were intended to prevent hot coals and clinkers from falling onto the hearth and were late versions of the rarely seen cover-fire or curfew, made of brass, which was used from medieval times for covering or extinguishing fires at night.

The mantelshelf, usually with a mirror over it, was adorned with candlesticks of pewter or brass, decorated tins and tea caddies, flashy vases, an occasional lustre mug or plate and in some cottages Staffordshire figures, those most free and vigorous products of popular art, modelled from illustrations and engravings by unlettered country potters with a simple sense of humour specially for the farmhouse and cottage mantelpiece. Amongst the ornaments on a battered chest of drawers in Mrs Holman's living room at Crewkerne were three fine Staffordshire figures – a large

61

149

154

Overleaf, left
151 Household gods in the living room of Mrs Holman's cottage at Crewkerne, Somerset.

Overleaf, right
152 *Above* Mrs Bowditch, senior, by her fireplace at Crewkerne, Somerset.

153 *Below left* Mantelpiece and cast-iron kitchen range (made locally) in Mrs Holman's living room at Crewkerne, Somerset.

154 *Below right* Interior at Lightmoor, Shropshire. The cottage was built in the early 18th century for an ironstone miner.

155 Interior with sideboard and table carpet in Mrs Tye's cottage at Little Barrington, Oxfordshire, the same room as that seen in Ill. 120.

156 Bedroom in Harthill Hall Farm, Alport, Derbyshire, showing a crude stone version of the double ogee hob grate, cottage chair of local joiner's design, washstand, and cast-iron bedstead with half tester. Note, in the window embrasure, the thickness of the wall.

spaniel and a pair of Highlanders – and an interesting portrait of Sir Francis Drake standing on a pedestal, of the type made at Liverpool in the early 19th century, together with two teapots, never used, each set in a fluted glass trifle dish, and a jug and basin. The last and the teapots with their sunken lids were typical of the Japanese imports which appeared in small country town shops in the early years of this century. The teapots were sold in wickerwork baskets intended to serve as tea cosies.

In front of the hearth there was often a coco mat or a rag rug in dark but glowing colours, and on it stood the armchairs of the cottager and his wife (she wearing a freshly laundered and starched apron, white, sprigged or spotted). The furniture usually included one or two older pieces, perhaps inherited but more often than not ousted by newer fashions from the 'big house' or the farmhouse. The chairs in Mr Moseley's cottage were a variety of the spindle back designed and made by a local carpenter. The sturdy chairs at Mrs Tye's, Little Barrington, with a single elaborately turned horizontal support, were examples of a type of which rural joiners made many spirited variations during the last century. The table was usually covered with patterned oil cloth, but when not in use it might be spread with a dark woollen cloth fringed by bobbles or tassels. At Mrs Tye's the table was resplendent with a carpet considered too good for the floor. Sideboards and 'what-nots', like the truly splendid one at Mrs Holman's, were frequently part of the cottage living-room furniture, and the occasional dresser might be quite imposing.

Cottage pictures, apart from photographs, most often consisted of Victorian oleographs or engravings. Three of the most popular subjects were *A World of Love* (a version of Edward Hicks's *The Peaceable Kingdom*), which hung above the sideboard at Mrs Tye's; *The Death of Nelson*, which 155 adorned the walls of old Mrs Bowditch's living room; and Landseer's *Death of the Stag*, which occupied much of the wall space in Mrs Giles's two-roomed cottage at Cricklade, Wiltshire. Cottages such as these nearly always contained a few books as well, which invariably included the Bible and very often the works of Tennyson and Bunyan's *Pilgrim's Progress*. In addition to these Mrs Tye owned *Raphael's Almanac* for 1952 and 1953 and a Victorian edition of *Robinson Crusoe*. Mrs Borrick of Grasmere had *The Death of Abel* (a translation of Gessner's poem), Milton's *Paradise Lost* and *Paradise Regained*, and a novel entitled *The Spiritual Quixote*, all on a broad window ledge among pots of geraniums.

Geranium plants, sometimes accompanied by begonias or calceolaria, VII, VIII stood in almost every cottage window, and they were specimens of conspicuous virility. Through them the cottagers could watch the doings of neighbours and the approach of strangers without themselves being seen.

Cottage bedrooms were still much like those described by Victorian observers – small, rather dark, normally without fireplaces and frequently opening one into another. If the bedroom had a fireplace it was usually of a standardized design in cast iron. Bedsteads were commonly of iron with 156 brass knobs. In addition to a dressing table many bedrooms were furnished with a Victorian washstand. Lace curtains hung at the window.

There were no bathrooms in the Essex farmhouses recorded in the sales catalogues I have mentioned, and remote and modest farmhouses were still without this convenience fifty or more years later. The cottages of farmhands were always at that time without it. A tin bath was often to be seen hanging behind the outshot door, and Mrs Holman's daughter described how it was brought onto the rug in front of the living room fire on a Friday night and what a luxury it was to sit in it beside the blazing grate with the oil lamp turned low.

The privies of cottages and of many farmhouses were outside, and at the bottom of the garden of one Northumberland homestead there were three seats in a row, all scrubbed snowy white.

And this brings me to the cottage garden, which now that rural labourers have almost ceased to live in cottages and are themselves so reduced in numbers only survive here and there. For those sophisticated flowery little plots, the work of retired ladies and urban invaders of the countryside inspired by the cultivation of the cottage garden by Miss Jekyll and William Robinson, enchanting though they so often are, do not belong to the artless tradition of the true cottager. The first essential characteristic of the genuine cottage garden is that it is not primarily ornamental: its charm is wholly unselfconscious and fortuitous. The cottager's garden was originally his family's larder, and so vegetables and flowers mingle together in it in happy proximity. The little plot in front of the cement-faced cottage with the engagingly brisk air at Knapton, Norfolk, noted in the last 124 chapter, preserved all the attributes of the true cottage garden as late as 1970. The path takes the shortest way to its goal, the front door, and is lined with flowers dividing it from neat rows of vegetables, an arrangement which is repeated again and again. A bed of onions makes an unpre-

157 *Above left* Front garden with miniature box hedge, Eriswell, Suffolk.

158 *Above right* Typical cottage garden displaying a mixture of vegetables and flowers at Knutsford, Cheshire.

meditated pattern among cushions of thyme, roses, Japanese anemones and Michaelmas daisies in front of a Victorian cottage near Knutsford, Cheshire; cabbages sprawl before a pargetted dwelling at Sibton, Suffolk, crowding out the flowers along the path, which here is of cinders. Where there is both a front and a back garden the cottager reserves the front for flowers while at the back vegetables are set in rows among gooseberry and redcurrant bushes and one or two fruit trees. Among them there may be a rabbit hutch and a wired fowl run.

The flowers may yet be of the old-fashioned varieties – native honeysuckle which owed its domestication to 16th-century cottagers, Turk's cap lilies and Madonna lilies, poppies, wallflowers, pinks, violets and primroses in their season and clematis like that festooning the cottage 146 door at Uggeshall, first developed from Traveller's joy in 17th-century cottage gardens. Old-world roses still linger among the vegetables of the cottage garden – moss and cabbage roses, the monthly rose and a rose which a farm labourer of Malham called 'Glory to thee John', his name for Gloire de Dijon.

Very often the vegetables and flowers of a cottage garden or the path and 157 the plants may be separated by a miniature box hedge, as at Victoria Place, Eriswell, Suffolk. These trim little hedges embody the simplest form of a clipping and shaping art in which the cottager excelled. It is an art with a long tradition, for Gervase Markham wrote in 1614 of the square bed filled with a design of close-cut box as one of the most ancient of all English garden ornaments. He speaks also of hedges simulating battlements which support the leafy figures of beasts, birds, 'creeping things and shippes'. Just such a hedge will arrest the attention of anyone approaching the Yorkshire village of Kirkby Malham by road. Rising above a dry-stone wall in front of a row of cottages, it is cut into the shape of great castellations with the green growing forms of peacocks resting upon them. The fashion for landscape gardening destroyed most of the evergreen sculpture which once embellished the formal layouts surrounding great houses, but the art lived on in the rural labourer's garden, introduced to him perhaps by gardeners who, themselves cottagers, were employed in the domains of the nobility and used their skill to enrich their own little plots. Round and massive pillars of box flank the door of a cottage at Coddenham in Suffolk, topped by small, conventionalized Christmas tree shapes on circular bases which give the little house its name – The Firs. Cocks crow from the height of tall ringed columns of yew at Sapperton, Gloucestershire; and in Warwickshire a ragged bird of gigantic proportions perches unsteadily on a swaying ringed plinth at Lower Brailes, a village dominated by shapes of living green. Dog and cat confront one another on top of a thick, exceedingly smooth hedge at Leverstock Green, Hertfordshire, while at Chipping Campden in Gloucestershire a huge symbolic cross of yew presses against a stone cottage wall stretching right up to the eaves and shading door and window with its great protective arms.

The examples of green sculpture I have just described were all flourishing in the late 1960s. But the future of cottage garden topiary is as dark as that of every other rural craft. Though yew is of faster growth than

159 *Below left* Topiary cross and trimly clipped hedges at Chipping Campden, Gloucestershire.

160 *Below right* Folly garden, Downton, Wiltshire.

box it still takes more than fifteen years for an image like the Chipping Campden cross to reach its full sombre solidity; and it seems unlikely in our unstable, mobile society that either the new urban and urbanized owners of old cottages or the rural labourer in his council house would think of planting for a more distant future than four or five years.

These sculptures are the folk version of a once sophisticated art and the cottager also gave a final, refreshingly popular and naïve twist to another aristocratic cvmon, the folly. The gnomes and miniature lighthouses and windmills, the plaster rabbits and toadstools, the wheelbarrows filled with primroses, which were the last degraded suburban manifestation of the folly and the Picturesque, made their way to the cottage garden as communication between town and country became easier. At Madeley Court, Shropshire, where the Elizabethan gatehouse was turned into two dwellings for farm workers in the early 19th century, pixies and rabbits merely added a touch of whimsy to a cottage plot without changing its character. All too often, the cottage garden tradition is destroyed by a weak suburban Picturesque convention. But in Cornwall a lighthouse on a pebble-studded base between two identical windows in one of those tiny flower gardens against a wall, in which cottagers delight, has the visual intensity of a painting by Alfred Wallis; and at Downton, Wiltshire, miniature pebble-encrusted steps inlaid with bits of china and with raised, rounded mosaics of pebbles and tiles like little cakes, leading up to a miniature pebble church amid tobacco plants, cabbages and leeks, create a composition as crazy and compelling and heart-warming as the ebullient little façade of the cottage at Wylye in the same county.

It is a wonderful ending to the Picturesque tradition that helped to undermine the vernacular tradition of which I have been writing and of which we have now seen the last. Old surviving farm buildings are no longer a reflection of working habits and have become objects of enthusiastic academic study; museums have been established to house old farm tools and implements and to preserve relics of the folklore and agricultural and village history of different regions. We live in a world where rural labourers have become mechanics, where the majority of farmers love profit more than they love the land, where agriculture has become an industry, farm buildings are products of the factory, and it is better not to contemplate what goes on inside them. Yet viewed in a wider context the scene is not without a glimmer of light. The influence of ecologists with comprehensive insight is daily growing. It may achieve a compromise between industry and agriculture and a general acceptance of the great metaphysical truth expressed by Bacon's dateless words: 'Nature cannot be commanded except by being obeyed.'

160

123

Further Reading

Besides the books mentioned in the Foreword, and the contemporary sources and probate inventories quoted in the text, the following publications illuminate various aspects of the subject:

Batsford, H. and Fry, C. *The English Cottage*, 1938
Billett, Michael *Thatching and Thatched Buildings*, 1979
Bourne, George *Change in the Village*, 1955 ed.
Briggs, M.S. *The English Farmhouse*, 1953
Campbell, Mildred *The English Yeoman under Elizabeth and the Early Stuarts*, 1942
Charles, F.W.E. *Medieval Cruck Building and its Derivatives*, 1967
Clifton Taylor, A., and Brunskill, R.W. *English Brickwork*, 1977
Collins, E.J.T. *From Sickle to Combine*, 1970
Emmison, F.G. *Jacobean Household Inventories*, Beds. Hist. Record Soc., XX, 1938
Ernle, Lord *English Farming Past and Present*, 1912

Evans, George Ewart *The Farm and the Village*, 1969
Fussell, G. *Robert Loder's Farm Accounts*, Camden Soc., 1936
—— *The English Rural Labourer*, 1952
Harris, Richard *Discovering Timber-framed Buildings*, 1977
Hasbach, W.A. *A History of the English Agricultural Labourer*, 1894, reprinted 1966
Havinden, M.A. *Household and Farm Inventories in Oxfordshire*, 1966
Hoskins, W.G. *The Midland Peasant*, 1957
Howitt, William *The Rural Life of England*, 1838
Jewell, Andrew (ed.) *Victorian Farming, a Sourcebook*, 1975
Jones, Sidney R. *English Village Homes and Country Buildings*, 1936
McHardy, D.N. *Modern Farm Buildings*, 1932

Mercer, E. *English Vernacular Houses*, 1975
Orwin, C.S., and Whetham, E.H. *History of English Agriculture 1846–1914*, 1967
Salzman, L.F. *Building in England down to 1500*, 2nd ed., 1967
Smith, J.T. 'Aisled Halls and their Derivatives', *Archaeological Journal*, 112, 1955
Steer, Francis *Farm and Cottage Inventories of Mid-Essex 1635–1749*, 1950
Tate, W.E. *The English Village Community and the Enclosure Movement*, 1967
Thirsk, Joan *English Peasant Farming*, 1957
—— 'Tudor Enclosures', *Historical Association*, 1959
——, and Imray, Jean (eds.) *Suffolk Farming in the Nineteenth Century*, 1958
Walton, J. *Homesteads of the Yorkshire Dales*, 1947
West, T. *Timber-framed Houses in England*, 1971

Index

Page numbers in *italic* indicate illustrations.
New county locations are given in brackets.